AMERICAN GUIDE TO U.S. COINS

AMERICAN GUIDE TO U.S. COINS

1972 EDITION

By Charles F. French

TRIDENT PRESS NEW YORK

This book is published by arrangement with
Cornerstone Library, Inc. and was produced
for Cornerstone Library, Inc. by Lyle and George Engel.

SBN: 671-27080-X

Library of Congress Catalog Card Number: 70-144780

Published simultaneously in the United States and Canada
by Trident Press, a division of Simon & Schuster, Inc., 630
Fifth Avenue, New York, N.Y. 10020

Printed in the United States of America

CONTENTS

Preface

The American Guide to U.S. Coins has been published annually as a paperback by Cornerstone Library since 1964. It is extremely gratifying to see this 1972 edition published for the first time as a hardcover book under the Trident Press imprint.

In my Prefaces to previous editions I stated that there is no list of actual coin values; all are estimates and prices change weekly. This is, of course, true although there are many fine books giving values. The values I have listed here are approximate and are gathered from advertised offerings, several trend valuations, and auction records. In order to keep constantly up to date, one must follow the market continuously.

In addition to current coin values, I have endeavored to give a brief history of American Numismatics from its earliest times to date. The first thirteen chapters are devoted to background and history, and from chapters 14 through 20 you will find practical advice for both the beginner and the advanced collector.

It is my hope that annual editions of this guide will continue to be published for many years to come.

CHARLES F. FRENCH

AMERICAN GUIDE TO U.S. COINS

Part One:

SOME HISTORY AND SOME ADVICE

INTRODUCTION: A BRIEF HISTORY OF AMERICAN NUMISMATICS

The discovery in 1843 of the celebrated 1804 silver dollar is one of the earliest indications we have of interest in numismatics. While there is a great deal of discussion regarding this coin's authenticity, it is generally agreed that the earliest were struck with the revision of Mint operations during the 1836–40 period. From 1858 on, the United States Mint struck proofs for collectors and, although not many of these were issued, this shows that there was considerable numismatic interest at that time.

The middle of the nineteenth century saw great interest in revising our coinages. It was the policy of the Mint to strike "trial" or experimental coins, and there appeared such unusual denominations as two-cent, three-cent, and twenty-cent pieces, none of which met with much popularity in circulation. They therefore were ultimately discontinued. Trial pieces became very popular with collectors in the 1860s and 1870s and it is possible that a good many of these were struck purely for the delight of the collector. Usually only a dozen or so patterns were needed, but quantities up to five hundred of some were struck.

The latter part of the nineteenth century saw the start of the American Numismatic Association and the publishing of America's first monthly magazine devoted exclusively to numismatics. "Students" came into being who ardently studied their particular field and many books of value were published towards the end of the century. The majority of these books were about cents and half cents; other topics covered were Colonial coins, half dimes, quarters, halves, and dollars. The popularity of large cents explains why there were so many publications about these interesting coins.

The following authors were pioneers in their subjects and paved the way for the many publications that have since appeared: Ebenezer Gilbert, Ed Frossard, Sylvester Crosby, W.W. Hays, Thomas Elder, F.W. Doughty, George H. Clapp, H.R. Newcomb, H.P. Newlin, D.W. Valentine, A.W. Browning, J.W. Haseltine, M.L. Beistle, Dr. M.W. Dickeson, Dr. Edward Maris, Philip Nelson, Sydney P. Noe, Carl Wurzbach, and Miller-Ryder.

There is no accurate record of the number of collectors in those days, but I would estimate that they must have numbered between three and five thousand. There were no "coin boards" or "plastic holders." Collectors had to improvise. The wealthier had wooden cabinets built, fitted with velvet-lined trays; others lined cigar boxes with velvet and placed their coins in these. Many a pleasant hour was spent going over coin collections, pointing out prized pieces to friends. Trading and exchanging coins with fellow numismatists became "the" thing to do.

Probably the first "coin holders" to become popular were the small round cardboard "pill" boxes manufactured by T. James Clarke of Jamestown, New York. Mr. Clarke, being a well-known collector of large cents, sold these boxes as containers for large cents, for they were just the right size. Collectors would put cotton in the bottom of the box, place the coin upon it, and write its description on the cover.

At the beginning of the twentieth century, coin collecting was a hobby only for the few deeply interested in the subject. There were perhaps ten thousand collectors at this time. They formed a national "clique" deeply interested in coin research, finding great new rarities and new varieties. One of the first accidental boons to the hobby was the issue of several million Columbian half dollars during the World's Fair at Chicago in 1892. This was the first coin struck in America commemorating an event and offered for sale to all. It opened the eyes of millions to the possibilities of coin collecting and showed how it could be interesting and even profitable. Collectors fondly kept those commemorative memoirs "to *coin* a phrase" of the World's Fair. The success of this first commemorative encouraged the issue of many more from 1900 on; while these kept the hobby active, they did not materially increase the number of collectors.

In the middle of the 1920s, the largest coin dealer was B. Max Mehl, who used the radio and national newspaper advertising to foster the sale of his new and excellent coin book. This book gave dealers the buying prices for all United States coins and also had many articles of interest on coins from all parts of the world, plus information about coin collecting. The book was a truly educational volume. It cost him thousands of dollars to advertise but, since he sold hundreds of thousands of books at a dollar each, we suspect he didn't lose any money. Mehl's coin book helped give the public a new awareness of numismatics, an awareness that was so far-reaching that even today we occasionally hear his great slogan, "I'll give fifty dollars for a 1913 Liberty-Head nickel." In fact, it was B. Max Mehl who made the 1913 nickel such a popular and desirable coin.

Up to the depression of 1929–33, coin values had gradually increased, as had new coin collectors. I would estimate that in 1930 there were probably twenty thousand coin collectors, many of them hard-pressed for money due to the depression. During those years collectors' coins could be purchased very reasonably. With the return of prosperity, a new stimulus came to numismatics. The many new issues of commemorative coins in 1935 and 1936 caused coin speculation on a large scale for the first time. Easy profits brought the speculator into the field. Commemorative prices skyrocketed and all United States coins were affected; values rose substantially. As might have been expected, when commemoratives crashed in 1937–38 many of the fast-buck boys lost interest in the hobby.

The first auction sales took place very early in the nineteenth century. There were only one or two well-known coin auctioneers. Toward the latter part of the 1930s, many new auctioneers went into the business. I still have a letter from a well-known dealer and auctioneer, Thomas Elder, bemoaning the fact that with all the auctions being conducted and coins being offered, prices would surely crash and coins become valueless. If only he had lived to see what has occurred and how greatly the hobby has grown.

In the beginning of the 1940s, many coin-minded people were confident of the future of numismatics. They reasoned that if the number of collectors continued to increase and there were no more coins to be had, prices would rise. They began accumulating uncirculated rolls of current coins against future demands. These investors would secure the rolls at their banks, or send away to dealers who specialized in this kind of business, and store them in safe deposit boxes. Uncirculated rolls were excellent investments, for how could one lose? At worst, the coins could be deposited in their bank at face value. Those that held these rolls long enough made small fortunes.

During the depression, the Whitman Publishing Company first put on the market an attractive, reasonably priced series of coin boards designed to encourage new collectors. They showed the novice what and how to collect, mostly, from his pocket change, and were offered throughout the United States in many kinds of stores. They steadily increased the number of coin collectors and are still a major factor in encouraging new ones.

Another great boon to numismatics was the resumption of the manufacture of proof sets in 1936 by the United States Mint in Philadelphia. Very few proofs and sets were sold from 1936 through 1942 and none were made during the war years of 1943–49. The record of the number of proof sets coined from 1950 on clearly indicates their increasing popularity. When one considers that there were 51,386 sets coined in 1950 and 3,950,762 in 1964, the answer is obvious as to the interest in coin collecting as a hobby.

Many people ask "Why do collectors like proof sets?" The first answer comes when you consider the care and accuracy with which they are coined and their beautiful mirror-like sheen. Second, there is a great appeal to collecting a series. Third, their value has constantly increased and they have been an excellent investment in the past.

Probably one of the greatest boons in recent years has been the introduction of coin newspapers, weekly and biweekly publications that reach all coin collectors, dealers and even people who are only remotely interested in coins. Shortly after the first issue of the coin newspapers, their circulation was in the hundred thousands; this was a great surprise to all "old time" numismatists, many of whom did not realize how wide the interest in numismatics had become.

A recent innovation is the advertised "bid" and "ask" prices, by dealers, of uncirculated rolls, proof sets, and commemoratives. These give the collector and investor an idea of current worths. Weekly published "coin trends" give an idea of how the market on all regularly issued coins is faring. For today's prices change very rapidly, sometimes up and sometimes down. Those interested are coin collectors of all classes, beginners, Whitman board collectors, speculators, investors, regular collectors, dealers, and students. The majority are new to the hobby and have a great deal to learn. The law of supply and demand governs prices. When the supply is short and demand great, values are bound to skyrocket. When certain pieces rise to very high prices, a great many small collectors are frozen out of the market for these particular coins. However, this only applies to coins that run well into the thousands of dollars per coin.

The American Numismatic Association conducts a national convention once a year in August held in various cities of the United States. Fifteen years ago, coin clubs began springing up throughout our country, today there are very few cities of respectable size that do not have their own clubs. They meet, usually once a month, conduct their business meetings, have talks on numismatics, occasionally conduct a club auction, buy and sell coins, and even have displays. They are always interested in gaining new members.

The large number of collectors and clubs has encouraged the forming of regional associations and you will find that these associations cover practically the entire country. Joined by clubs and collectors in their regional territory, these associations hold either one or two conventions per year. Many have auction sales conducted during their convention and a bourse where dealers from all over the United States congregate to offer their coins for sale. Collectors are encouraged to display their collections and are awarded prizes for their efforts on a competitive basis.

Numismatics today is well organized. Since its start, the latter part of the nineteenth century, the American Numismatic Association has grown slowly and steadily until its membership is well over thirty thousand. Under this parent organization come the regional associations and then the local coin clubs. In addition to the above, there is the American Numismatic Society in New York City, which maintains an outstanding museum of rare coins. The society has a remarkable library and issues many new publications, devoting its efforts to research.

1. EARLY AMERICAN COINS

Were we to transport ourselves back three centuries to the early days of Colonial America, we would find that industry was very small and that business, for the most part, was conducted by barter and trade. While the need of coins was felt, the shortage was not as important as later, when Colonial America became more industrialized and succeeded in acquiring wealth. Even so, attempts to issue coins were made.

Massachusetts experimented with its NE (New England) shillings, sixpence, and threepence. These very crude and rare coins are credited with being the first coins struck in the territories then known as the American Colonies.

Following quickly came the Willow, Oak, and Pine Tree series. Some were to find use in circulation, for in those days a coin was a coin regardless of who issued it, and the amount of metal it contained determined its value. This first series was strongly disapproved of by Charles II of England, and the coinage was stopped.

There were other very early experiments in coinage in other Colonies. The Mark Newby halfpence, struck in Dublin in 1678, was originally coined for Ireland but found its way to New Jersey. There were also the Lord Baltimore pieces for Maryland, which were coined in England and brought over for circulation here.

After these early attempts, we find little activity numismatically until the first part of the eighteenth century, when a small flurry again occurred. We have the Gloucester tokens of 1714, and the Wood or Hibernia series and Rosa Americana coins of 1722 and 1724. There were the early French Colony coppers of 1721–22; and a little earlier, the Elephant tokens of 1694. With the exception of the Gloucester tokens, of which little is known, the rest were struck in foreign lands and shipped here for use, due to the dire need. The Higley, or Granby, coppers of 1737–39 saw considerable circulation, even though they were unauthorized and coined on this continent.

As we enter the second period of inactivity, the 1767 French Colony pieces, with the exception of the 1760 Voce Populi coins, find little or no interest in "coins for America." The next and most important era commenced around the time of our embarking on the American Revolution. From this time until the opening of the first United States Mint, in 1792–93, we find innumerable varieties, experiments, in fact all types of coins. Some received recognition and actually circulated. Others should be classified as pattern or experimental pieces. Of these I shall first discuss the State cents.

New Hampshire, as early as 1776, struck coppers. As shown by their great amount of wear, they must have circulated considerably, even though very few are known. Vermont issued many varieties and quite a few cents from 1785 through 1788, and they were actively used in circulation. New York, too, issued cents from 1786 through 1787, some of which could be considered experimental pieces, others actually circulated. Connecticut probably had the most active coinage system from 1785 through 1788. All of her coins were circulated extensively. Massachusetts struck some early experimental pieces around 1776 and went into regular coinage during 1787 and 1788. New Jersey issued a wide variety of cents from 1786 through 1788. Virginia, in 1773, struck pennies and halfpennies with George III on them.

During this time, just prior to the Revolution, a wide variety of experimental coins or tokens appeared. The majority did not see circulation even though some are known to have been used. In this group we find the rare pewter pattern Continental dollars of 1776; the Nova Constellatio coppers of 1783–85–86; the

Immune Columbia pieces, the Confederatio cents; Brasher's experimental pieces, and Chalmers Annapolis (Maryland) shillings, sixpence, and threepence. Belonging here, too, are the U.S.A. Bar cents, Mott tokens, Talbot, Allum, and Lee tokens, Georgius Triumpho tokens, Auctori Plebis tokens, Kentucky tokens, Myddleton tokens, North American tokens, Pitt tokens, Rhode Island Ship tokens, and Franklin Press cents.

Now we come to what may be the forerunners of our first regular coinage, the Washington pieces. George Washington's great popularity at the end of the Revolution made it natural to want to copy the practice of foreign nations and place the head of the ruler on the obverse of the coin. There being no "ruler" of the United States, the president was the logical equivalent. If this practice had been accepted and carried out until today, we would have had a change in coin design with each president; the bust or head of each president would have appeared on our coins while he was in office. This would have been an interesting series for our coin collectors, but the many changes might very possibly have confused our coinage. (This frequent changing of coin designs did not occur in kingdoms, for the rulers were in for life.)

The practice of using Washington's head was therefore discarded and the Liberty-Head designs adopted. Many of the designs from Washington pieces, however, were adopted either partly or entirely.

The reverse of the Unity cents of 1783 is almost identical to the reverse design adopted on the wreath-type cents of 1793 and the following years. The eagle on the reverse of the various cents and half dollars is very similar to the eagle adopted for the reverse of our silver coins.

The designs of the half disme, disme, Birch cent, and silver-center cents are almost identical to the designs adopted on our coins of 1793. The Fugio cents of 1787 which actually saw circulation, while authorized by Congress, were coined privately.

You will notice that all of the above were coinages designed to fill the need of minor coins, mostly cent and half-cent sizes; this was the size that was needed most. Business requirements in larger transactions were carried on in gold Spanish-American doubloons and their fractions, English guineas, and even French louis d'or. Silver requirements were largely supplied by the masses of one-, two-, four-, and eight-real coins of Spanish America.

2.

PIRATE AND REVOLUTIONARY MONEY

Our coasts were infested with pirates and privateers during the early days of our Colonial History. This made shipping hazardous and uncertainty was the order of the day. British, French, and particularly Spanish ships were liable to be boarded, stripped of their cargo and then sunk. With the exception of the Spaniards shipping gold and silver treasure back to Spain other cargoes usually consisted of articles sorely needed by settlers in the new world; guns, ammunitions and luxuries desired by the rich.

Gold and silver were not always in coin form for bullion was found to be more easily handled.

The Spaniards lost many ships of treasure, either through pirate raids or sunk by hurricanes. Gold coins, subjected to the action of salt water are not harmed at all, neither are rare jewels, but silver is badly affected by the corrosive action of the salt and these must be treated carefully to remove the corrosion and encrustations they acquire after centuries of lying under salt water.

During the American Revolution, the need for hard money was so great in the United States that it encouraged our authorizing private shipowners to turn "pirate." Known as privateers, these sleek fast ships roved our coast and captured any ship they could as a prize of war, placing their American crews on them and sending them to the Colonies. For the ship captains and owners this was a very lucrative business and many of the wealthy clipper ship owners of the next fifty years started out in this manner. The wealth of unobtainable material these privateers brought to the revolting Colonies was of terrific aid to the successful consummation of the war. Not only were goods brought to our shores, but a sorely needed quantity of hard money. Many English gold guineas were confiscated as they were being shipped over to the continent to pay English armies.

We must try to visualize the situation of that day in order to realize the need of this money. The early Americans had always considered hard coins the only money of real value; gold coins were used for business transactions of merit. It made no difference from what country the coins came as long as they were coins; this also applied to silver and copper. The dire needs of the war caused the individual colonies to issue paper currency, which was not looked upon with much favor.

When the Continental Congress began issuing paper currency to pay bills, their money was looked down upon and inflation swept the country to a degree that almost wrecked the war efforts. The expression "Not worth a Continental" comes to us from those days when everyone shied away from these bills. They never were redeemed and finally became of no value. For the most part, however, the earlier notes issued by the individual colonies were redeemed, but in varying percentages of their face value. To aggravate the situation further, the British resorted to counterfeiting our paper money and attempting to circulate it.

3.

GOLD DOLLARS AND GOLDEN EAGLES

Prior to the establishment of our United States Mint, a proposal was made, in 1785, to coin five-dollar pieces, but the actual approval of our first gold pieces did not come until 1792 when Congress passed an act authorizing the coinage of eagles ($10.00), half eagles ($5.00), and quarter eagles ($2.50). The eagles were to be 247½ grains pure, 270 grains standard. Half eagles were to be 123¾ pure, 135 grains standard; quarter eagles were to be 61⅞ pure, 67½ grains standard. The standard weight included an alloy to make the coins wear better.

These gold coins were pegged to silver on a 15 to 1 ratio, namely fifteen ounces of silver to one ounce of gold, and while this ratio was all right at the time the bill was passed, by 1799 the ratio in Europe had reached 15¾ to 1, and the overvalued gold coins began to flow out of the country or were melted down to get the extra value they contained. Gold therefore disappeared from circulation, as did silver dollars.

It wasn't until June 28, 1834, that a new law reduced the weight of gold coins. From that time on, our gold pieces appeared in the new smaller size, returned to circulation, and created a new interest in and demand for gold. Gold mines profitably increased their production. Our mint first struck twenty-dollar double eagles, and experimented with fifty-dollar coins in 1849. We also find our first gold dollars appearing, closely followed by threes. The three-dollar gold piece, first coined in 1854, was never a popular coin. It was frequently linked with bad luck by the superstitious.

The quantities of gold and shortages of gold coins in the west prompted the coinage of pioneer pieces in many denominations. Privately issued and not under rigid regulations, many of these were not up to standard fineness; as late as the latter part of the 1920s these pioneer pieces were looked down upon as low-grade, undervalued coins and were redeemed by financial institutions at less than face value. Today, these low-grade coins are rare and worth high premiums, not for their gold value but for their numismatic value.

From the time shortly after the Civil War until the banking holiday in 1933, numismatic interest in collecting gold coins was not high, perhaps because of the coins' face value. Anyone who wanted to collect them could easily have secured the majority of all denominations for very little over face value, even back to 1834, when the new smaller size was adopted. A great many of the first gold pieces prior to 1804 could have been purchased for much less than their rarity should have dictated.

Proof gold coins were not popular with collectors. With the exception of the last few years, only twenty-five to forty proof gold dollars have been struck each year! Similar small quantities were coined in proofs for quarter eagles, threes, half eagles, eagles, and double eagles. The largest quantity of gold proof dollars of any year were struck in 1889, and this only amounted to 1,779 pieces! The majority of proofs struck in all denominations per year usually ran from twenty to forty specimens! Over ten times that amount or more were struck for coins in silver and copper. It is no wonder that perfect proof gold pieces bring very high prices today.

Due to the depression of 1929–33 and the uncertainty of the country's financial position, hoarding of gold coins by individuals became so common it seriously endangered our financial structure. This was one of the major reasons for the government order that all gold coins be turned in. The purpose of this order was to end hoarding and get gold back where it could do the country more good. The first announcement of the government order was widely publicized and stressed the penalties for failure to comply, which at the time were drastic, with stiff jail sentences. The order accomplished what it intended and millions of dollars in gold coin were deposited in banks and Federal Reserves.

It is regrettable that, because of the hysteria of the time, many really rare gold coins were turned in. The government was not interested in the coins themselves, but only in hoards. Within a few weeks the original order, which exempted gold coins in quantities of $100 was amended to exempt gold coins that were considered rare and held in coin collections. Over a period of years subsequent amendments gradually continued to ease the stringency of the original order. At first limits were lifted with the exception of two-and-one-half-dollar pieces. Restrictions on the two-and-one-half-dollar pieces limited ownership to not more than two of any date or mint mark. This restriction was lifted next and the offense was changed from a criminal to a civil one with a fine. One restriction still in effect forbids importing into this country any gold coins struck by foreign nations dated from 1933 to date, insofar as these coins probably were not designed for circulation.

Since the Hoarding Act of 1933, interest in gold coin collecting has been growing by leaps and bounds. As soon as the government discontinued making gold coins, collectors began taking great interest in them.

There are no restrictions regarding the export or import, purchase, sale, or collecting of gold coins in the United States dated before 1933.

4.

PRIVATE GOLD COINS

Necessity has brought into reality many things, and so, through a necessity, we have our private territorial gold coins. These pieces were issued between 1830 and 1862 in different parts of our country to answer a demand for denominations lacking in regular issues. While there were laws that forbade the individual states striking gold coins, there were none forbidding private persons or private companies doing so.

In 1787, the year before Washington was elected to the presidency, a jeweler named Ephraim Brasher, whose place of business was on Cherry Street in New York City, appealed to the state legislature for permission to strike copper coins to circulate in that state. Permission was refused, but that did not stop him from using the dies he had made. He struck his coins in gold, their intrinsic value being $16, the same as the Spanish doubloons. They were known as the Ephraim Brasher doubloons. The one with EB on the right wing of the eagle is one of the highest priced coins in the world.

The years 1830–40 saw great industrial development and territorial expansion in our country. The first steam locomotive, streetcar, and omnibus were put to use; the Erie Canal was built and the telegraph invented.

In 1830, a treaty with Great Britain opened to American commerce the ports of the West Indies and South America; a treaty with Turkey opened the Black Sea. Around the same time, Templeton Reid, assayer, located near the gold mines in Lumpkin County, Georgia, issued the first of his private gold coins. It is not definitely known just how long his business existed or just when it started, but the first coins to bear his stamp were dated 1830. The coins issued from his Georgia establishment contained gold of a higher standard and fineness than any other ever issued by either private persons or the government. It is reasonable to assume that this is why so many were melted, resulting in their great scarcity.

Christopher Bechtler's establishment was located in Rutherford County, North Carolina. The first of his coins, although undated, are attributed to the early part of 1831. About 1842, he passed his business on to his son August, who continued until about 1852. The gold for these pieces came from North Carolina and Georgia.

When Texas was admitted to the Union as an independent state, arbitration over the boundary resulted in the war with Mexico and ended with the Treaty of Guadeloupe in 1848. For $18,000,000 Mexico sold all of her northern territory to the United States. This territory included the region known as California, Utah, Nevada, New Mexico, and part of Colorado and Arizona.

Civilization had already pushed its way westward when the cry of "gold" came from California and resounded from coast to coast. There was a great exodus from the east; people poured into the west in droves. The trials and hardships of the cross-country trek with inadequate means did not stop them. With the influx of prospectors, traders, merchants, and people from every walk of life, towns grew up overnight. It was the dawn of a Golden Age. The forty-niner was staking his claim.

The discovery of gold in California was a boon to a world suffering from a gold shortage. It changed the whole outlook of industry and commerce. Prices skyrocketed to unbelievable heights. For a while gold dust was used as a medium of exchange, but this was soon found to be cumbersome and impractical. The demand for gold coins was great but there were no mints in the west. To ship gold dust to the east to be minted into coins was out of the question. Besides not having adequate means for shipping, there were the hazards of holdups, Indians, and slow progress overland. An attempt was made by the provincial government in the Oregon Territory to establish a mint, but this failed. A private organization, the Oregon Exchange Company, started operations in Oregon City in 1849. They employed a blacksmith to make the apparatus and an engraver, who happened to be one of the company's members, to make the dies.

The Mormons, who for years had been migrating westward, having been expelled from New York, Illinois, and Nebraska, finally settled on the shores of the Great Salt Lake in Utah, while it was still Mexican territory. They started their mint in 1849, striking coins from the gold dust received from California. Their twenty-dollar gold piece was the first to be struck in this country, but the intrinsic value was found to be only between $16 and $18.

There were about fifteen private mints operating in California between 1849 and 1855, striking millions of dollars worth of gold coins. Norris, Greig & Norris coined the first, a five-dollar coin of 1849; Moffat & Company struck the first ten-dollar coin; Baldwin & Company, the first twenty; Moffat & Company, the first fifty. The fifty-dollar coin was octagonal, bearing the stamp of the United States Assayer Augustus Humbert. F.D. Kohler & Company and Moffat & Company issued ingots stamped from gold bars. The last private issue coins from California came from the mints of Wass, Mollitar & Company and Kellogg & Company, dated 1855, just one year after the San Francisco Mint was opened.

In 1857 a panic overtook the country due to over-capitalization, over-building of railroads, rise of prices, speculation, bad crops, bad state banking, and diminishing gold output. While there was agitation between the states over the question of states' rights and the Dred Scott Decision, the first Atlantic cable was being laid. Silver was discovered in Nevada and a new gold district was discovered in the west. The forty-niner rush was repeated but not in the same proportions as the rush a decade before; the states' rebellion had become a serious issue.

There were three private minting firms in Colorado. The first coins to be struck were by Clark, Gruber & Company, in 1860. Coins of all United States gold denominations with the exception of ones and threes were issued. In 1862, the government purchased the Clark, Gruber establishment, which was thereafter conducted as a United States Assay Office. The original bill called for a government mint at Denver, but this did not materialize until 1906.

John Parsons & Company, Tarryall Mines, and J.J. Conway & Company, Georgia Gulch, operated their private mints at about the same time for a limited period. Parsons issued quarter eagles and half eagles; Conway, quarter eagles, half eagles, and eagles. None of the coins bore dates, but they are said to have been struck in 1861. All are quite rare, Conway's exceedingly so.

The designs on these privately issued gold coins are varied. Some are very plain with only the name of the mint or minter, date, and denomination or weight. Others have very attractive original designs, and still others are so very much like the regular government coinage that to the ordinary layman they are easily mistaken.

5.
THE COINS OF THE MORMONS

"During the year 1846, the beginning of the great exodus from Nauvoo, Illinois, to Salt Lake Valley, Utah, there appeared a strange little brass token that has created and attracted the attention of church members and collectors from all over the country" (*Numismatist*, July, 1911, p. 241). The date and Brigham Young's favorite emblem—the beehive, meaning "Let everyone do his duty," and clasped hands, signifying friendship—indicate very strongly that the coin is associated with the Mormons. However, some believe that it is in no way connected with the Mormons, because the emblem of the beehive was first thought of after their arrival in the valley. We do not know whether this token was used as an exchange medium or as a commemorative issue, nor do we know what its value was. Its size was about that of a dime.

When the Mormons went west, they took very little money with them and droughts, insects, and other adverse conditions drained what money they had. Hard work ultimately conquered all their handicaps and eventually Indians were no longer a threat. Trade and barter were their mediums of exchange. A Mormon battalion in the Mexican War brought home with them, in 1847, a certain amount of money which circulated. It is recorded that Captain James Brown left the valley in 1847 to collect his men's back pay, returning with $5,000 in Spanish gold doubloons valued at $16 each. Many other instances of small quantities of coin coming into the hands of the Mormons are on record, but the discovery of gold in the ground was the start of a desire to issue coins.

A very interesting and integral part of the Mormons' history was contributed by Thomas Rhoads, more commonly referred to as Father Rhoads. Rhoads and his family left Missouri in the spring of 1846 for Sutter's Fort on the Sacramento River. Upon arriving at the fort, Rhoads and his five sons signed up for service in the Mexican War. After termination of their services they returned to Sutter's Fort just in time to help organize a party for the purpose of rescuing a snowbound Donner party trapped in the California mountains. The small rescue party was successful in its attempt to locate the lost Donner party, but unfortunately did not arrive in time to save the group from starvation. Only a few members of the Donner party survived.

On their way home, hunger once again reared its ugly head, for the bears had eaten the supplies that members of the rescue party had tied to the trees to aid them on their return trip. The party finally reached civilization once again, but not before scarcity of food compelled them to eat the rawhides from their snowshoes.

When gold was discovered in the channel of the mill race at Sutter's Sawmill, Rhoads and his sons joined the other adventurers in their quest for gold, which later proved very rewarding. After accumulating a small fortune, Rhoads and his family left

California for Great Salt Lake in the latter part of 1848. News of the Rhoads fortune leaked out and while they were making their way through the California mountains they were attacked by bandits. Had it not been for the intervention of some passing travelers, the ambush might have been successful. With the help of the travelers, the Rhoads family was able to repel the attack.

According to Colonel Lock, Father Rhoads brought with him several sacks of gold, among which there was a 60-pound sack, the largest amount that had been brought into the valley. Father Rhoads turned all the gold over to Brigham Young, who in return had a home built for Rhoads and allowed him to withdraw from the tithing office all the food supplies that he deemed necessary. Rhoads also received a herd of cattle in consideration for the gold dust. It was customary for each individual to give one-tenth of his accomplishments to the church, whether cattle, produce, or money, in order to aid their common cause. But Father Rhoads contributed his entire amount in order to accelerate the progress of the Mormon people. The famous 60-pound sack of gold was the chief topic of the people in the valley at that time and for quite some time to come.

Concerning gold dust that was brought into the valley, William T. Fullett, a battalion member, was credited with having made the first deposit on December 10, 1848. He deposited fourteen and one-half ounces of gold dust which was then worth $232, equal to $16 per ounce. Within four months, close to $8,000 in dust and a little coin was deposited in the "bank." Entries of deposit show that battalion men deposited 77 percent, and 135 others, 35 percent of the total.

Since the city was fairly well supplied with gold dust, the council unanimously agreed that it was time to convert the dust into coins. In order to accomplish this, President Young solicited the aid of John Kay and John Taylor in planning the first mint ever to be established in the Great Salt Lake Valley.

John Kay, skilled in patternmaking, and John Taylor were persuaded to work on suitable designs for the coins. After some time and difficulty, the preparations were finally completed and Kay began to melt the gold and roll it into sheets. A punching press was then used in punching out the gold discs, while a coining press stamped the designs on the discs.

Kay turned out ten-dollar pieces which were paid out at a premium of fifty cents on the piece. Whether the coins were at a premium because of the novelty value or because of overweight is not known. Twenty of them were charged out to Brigham Young and five to John Kay. A week later twenty-one pieces were coined and charged out at par to Brigham Young. No more were coined until September, 1849, because the crucibles were broken in the preliminary runs and melting could not be continued until others were obtained.

Since the coining could not be continued, the punching press was dismantled and shipped by ox team to Parowan where it could be put to use while the crucibles were being made. During the short time the press was in Parowan, it was used for cutting nails. The sheet iron was cut into strips and then headed in a vise. On October, 1848, the press was returned to the valley where it was used in connection with the coinage of the 1849–50 gold coins and later, the 1860 gold coins.

Finally, the patternmaker Kay completed his work on refining the gold dust, and at last the mint was ready for operation. In order to test the crucibles, Kay struck a few pattern pieces bearing a design on only one side. This time the crucibles did not break. Apparently the workers were satisfied with the results, because the mint went into full production and remained so for the remainder of the year.

Joseph Fielding Smith, church historian, made the following statement concerning the men who participated in the coining of these gold coins:

> When the Desert Mint was built, Alfred B. Lambson forged all the dies and punches, in fact all that pertained to the mint with the exception of the drop hammer, which was forged by Martin H. Beck. John Kay cut the dies and coined the money, William Clayton and Thomas Bullock being associated with him as accountant and weigher. As an expedient, before this Dr. Willard Richards weighed the gold dust brought from California and placed it in small packages, representing from $1 to $20 which passed current for money.[1]

---

[1]By permission of the Church Historian, Church of Jesus Christ of Latter-Day Saints; reprinted from *Mormon Money* by Sheridan L. McGarry.

The designs on the pieces were not too elaborate, but one must admit originality and much praise should be forthcoming for the job they did with such limited facilities.

The following is a description of the gold coins minted in Salt Lake City: on the obverse in the center, there are clasped hands with the date 1849 below; the legend reads "G.S.L.C.P.G." (Great Salt Lake City Pure Gold), "Two and half Do." On the reverse is a crown over the all-seeing eye, around the edge of which are the words "HOLINESS TO THE LORD." The designs on the 1849 and 1859 coins were all the same with the exception of the 1850 five-dollar piece. This had nine stars around the edge and a slightly different crown.

It is generally believed that during the early coinage no effort was made to assay or refine the gold because there was no one connected with the mint capable of determining such standards. This fact has been substantiated by Captain H. Stansbury in his report on his exploration and survey of the Great Salt Lake. The coinage was done in good faith, however, because of the then prevailing theory of "relative fineness"; in other words, the Mormons based the worth of all gold upon the purity of California gold. Little did they realize that the coins minted from native gold were very low in assay due to the fineness of the gold, although it was full weight. According to Colonel Lock, the 1849 five-dollar gold piece was actually worth $4.51. This mistake was later brought to light but not before losses had been sustained by many who had purchased gold on the relative-fineness theory.

6. CIVIL WAR MONEY

Southern guns roared on Fort Sumter and the Civil War had begun. Our nation had started the bloodiest war in its history.

Patriotism ran high in the newly formed Confederacy, and the cry went out for all to help in the war effort by turning in their gold, silver, and other precious metals in exchange for both state and Confederate notes. Southern bonds were issued to finance the war–all with promises to pay a certain number of years after the ratification of peace between the North and South. There was no question about who would win–the South of course! And this temporary paper money was just as good as having the gold coins it represented–or so they thought.

Financing the war was no easy task. The South, not having much heavy industry of its own, had to rely on foreign aid for its sorely needed supplies–which it had to pay for with hard cash.

Coins soon went out of circulation. There was an attempt to continue operation of the New Orleans mint, but, due to lack of metal, this failed, and the only coins that were struck there for the Confederacy were the cent and half-dollar–both experimental pieces, and very rare. The Dahlonaga and Charlotte mints were closed for good.

As the war progressed and things began looking blacker, public confidence waned. There was a scramble for gold, and some state bank notes (formerly considered "as good as gold") were redeemed for gold at "20 cents on the dollar."

As more and more money was needed, more and more Confederate paper was printed. Great quantities were printed in 1864–the last year this paper money was issued. Printing presses were turning out denominations anywhere from fifty-cent notes up to five-hundred-dollar bills.

The collapse of the Southern effort put an end to this, and rendered all Confederate money valueless; the land was left destitute as a result. While much of the money was destroyed, some found its way into attics, in cartons and trunks, where it lay for decades–a useless reminder of the great war effort. Many stories have been told since of old Southern families with trunks full of Confederate money stored in their attics.

The vastly increased interest in numismatics over the past two decades has brought much of this currency out of its storage places. There are a few rarities in existence, such as the Montgomery, Alabama $1,000 and $500 notes, plus a few others, which are worth more today than their original face value. The majority, however, are worth less.

The start of the war in the North was quite different, however. Heavily industrialized, the North was far better equipped to cope with the problems presented by the war.

There too, small change soon went out of circulation. The loss of the New Orleans mint cut coin output in half, throwing the burden of coin manufacture on the shoulders of the Philadelphia and San Francisco mints. Although these mints were also hampered by the shortage of metal, they were not nearly as hard hit as the South.

Contributing to the great shortage of hard cash was the desire of many to hoard and the greatly increased need for small change in day-to-day business transactions. Housewives going to market were constantly plagued by a lack of change; merchants, therefore, were compelled to improvise methods of providing change, with the result that postage stamps were frequently used for this purpose. While a necessity, the use of stamps for this purpose was a nuisance since the stamps often stuck together, lost their gum (one reason why so many of our early issues are found in mint condition without gum), and were very fragile.

A year after the war began, a Mr. J. Gault patented the first encased postage stamps. This consisted of a round brassy metal frame in which stamps of various denominations were inserted and covered with a transparent mica cover. It protected the stamp, served the purpose of a coin and could be used much longer because of its cover. Denominations issued were for one, two, three, five, ten, twelve, twenty-four, thirty, and ninety cents.

The enterprising Mr. Gault arranged to have advertising placed on the back cover, and while many have his name on them, dozens of Northern firms paid to use this convenient method of providing change. Outstanding among these are such concerns as Ayers Pills, Drakes Plantation Bitters, Burnetts Cooking Extracts, Lord and Taylor, North American Insurance Co., etc. All of these encased postage stamps are quite rare–the highest-valued ones being those stamps in the higher denominations.

Another answer to the coin shortage was the series known as Civil War Tokens. They first appeared the latter part of 1861, and were coined in great quantities until 1864, when laws–still in effect today–abolished all *private* money coining. It is estimated that about fifty million of these tokens were coined during this period, in two main varieties: patriotic ones, with novel political legends–"our flag, should anyone tear it down, shoot him on the spot"; "millions for contractors, not one cent for widows", etc., and merchants' tokens, which appeared with legends advertising wares. Although these were not legitimate money, they were used as cents.

The war had caused the suspension of specie payments, and all coins had gone out of circulation; hoarding was universal. Copper-nickel cents of 1859–64 were worth a premium.

The situation was serious, something had to be done. In 1862, Congress passed a bill authorizing postage currency. Notes in denominations of 5c., 10c., 25c., and 50c., had facsimiles of the current 5c. and 10c. postage stamps printed on them. This was brought about by the wide use of postage stamps as small change. While not favored, the system was used.

In 1863, a new act was passed authorizing the first issue of Fractional Currency. This currency circulated until as late as 1876, when an act authorized its redemption in silver coin.

During 1866 and 1867, the Treasury Department made up special Fractional Currency shields. These were an ornate arrangement of specimen notes, printed on one side and framed. They included notes of all issues, both obverse and reverse, for the first three series. The 15c. Grant and Sherman notes were included, even though these never appeared in circulation. Shields were distributed to banks to assist them in detecting counterfeits. These shields are quite rare and difficult to find in good condition. Many were taken apart in the hope that the notes could be sold or spent.

Before the Civil War, State Bank charters were easy to obtain. The rapid expansion of our economy had created the need for more money and State Banks were authorized to issue paper money against their deposits. This system was satisfactory as long as there was prosperity; in recession, however, deposits were withdrawn, banks closed their doors, and money became valueless.

While paper money was looked upon with suspicion, the government was compelled to issue its first currency: the demand notes of 1861 and the legal tender notes of 1862 and 1863. Issued in denominations of from one dollar to one thousand dollars, they were called "greenbacks" from the color on the reverse side.

The one-dollar and two-dollar denominations were often sent to the "boys in blue" at the front. It became the practice to pin these notes to a heavy piece of paper so they could not be detected in the mails, and stolen. Many of the notes of this series we find today have these pin holes in them.

With the termination of hostilities, changes in minting procedures came about. In the South, the mint in New Orleans was not permitted to resume operations until 1879, and for over a decade it only issued silver dollars. In the West, a new mint was opened in 1870 at Carson City. The San Francisco mint continued to operate, turning out gold coins. The Philadelphia mint bore the brunt of our nation's small-change needs. As the economy gradually got back on a normal footing, change was again available in our pockets.

7.

HARD TIMES TOKENS

During the stirring period from 1832 to 1844, politics and the economy of the country produced the Hard Times Tokens.

President Andrew Jackson disapproved of a fiscal system under which public funds were deposited in a single, privately controlled institution—the Bank of the United States. In 1832 Jackson vetoed the bill to continue the Bank's existence after the expiration of its charter in 1836. This was in opposition to Clay and the financial interests of the country. This caused an upheaval in both political parties.

Jackson's party split into two opposed groups. And Clay's supporters fought to restore the bank. Jackson and his successor, Martin Van Buren, succeeded in warding off the attacks and put in reforms.

They discontinued depositing funds in the Bank of the United States and established a Sub-Treasury system. Metallic currency was the only medium of payment for public lands.

At the time the country was undergoing a severe depression. That, plus the uncertainty of the banking system, led to hoarding hard money. Paper money was so unreliable, nobody wanted to accept it. The demand on the large cent, and the disappearance of small change, led to the manufacture of the Hard Times Tokens. Those with political slogans were the first campaign tokens.

Some of the legends on the Political Tokens are as follows:

"Andrew Jackson President Elected 1828 re-elected 1832–We commemorate the glorious victories of our hero in war and in peace."

"Gulian C. Verplanck Our Next Govnr A Faithful friend of our Country."

Small bust of Jackson with "My Substitute for the U.S. Bank. My Experiment, My Currency, My Glory." A running boar: "My Victory, My third Heat, Down with the Bank, Perish Credit, Perish Commerce."

Running Jackass: "I follow in the steps of my illustrious predecessor." Turtle with strongbox on its back marked "Sub Treasury." "Executive Experiment."

Balking horse: "Constitution as I understand it," "Roman Firmness," "A Plain System Void of Pomp."

Jackson sitting in a strongbox with a sword and a bag of money: "I take the responsibility." Sailing vessel named "Constitution" wrecked: "Van Buren Metallic Currency."

Phoenix: "Substitute for shin-plasters," "Specie payments suspended May 10, 1837" in wreath.

Ship "Constitution" under full sail: "Webster credit Currency." Ship named "Experiment" wrecked on the rocks: "Van Buren Metallic Currency."

Slave tokens: "Am I Not a Man and Brother." Another: "Am I not a Woman and Sister."

There are many varieties of "Liberty Heads" similar to large United States cents. Some are very ugly. In addition to some of the reverses already mentioned they are also found with "Millions for Defense, Not One Cent for Tribute"; "Mint Drop Bentonian Currency"; "Mint Drop Benton Experiment"; Ugly Head obverse with "Loco Foco" instead of "Liberty" on headband.

Many enterprising merchants of the day issued tokens advertising their wares to be used as small change. Some of these tokens have the same obverses as the Political Tokens.

Others have the type of business on them—a clock-maker has a clock; a boot-maker, a boot; a barber, a comb and scissors. A gold-beater has an arm and sledge, an anvil represents hardware and cutlery. A circus rider on two horses stands for the Hippodrome, and a railroad coach for the New York and Harlem Railroad.

Edwin Parmele's liquor store has an inebriate with a glass. An agriculturist has a bull. An umbrella-maker has an open umbrella, and a chair-maker, an upright chair. Public baths are indicated by a nude.

Lyman H. Low listed 183 Hard Times and Merchants' Tokens from 1832 to 1844. While many are easily available, there are others which are rare.

They were made in bronze, brass, and white metal, the bronze being the commonest. The majority were made the size of large cents but there are a few of smaller.

8.
COMMEMORATIVE COINS

The opening of the Chicago World's Fair in 1892 was the occasion for the issue of our first commemorative coins, the Columbian half dollars. Designed to help defray expenses, they did not at first meet with great enthusiasm. A good many were coined in 1892 and still more in 1893. It was hoped that nearly 2,500,000 of both dates could be sold at one dollar each.

Many were sold, brought home by visitors, and kept for years as souvenirs of the exposition. A great many, however, did not sell and ultimately were placed in circulation at face value. For many years it was not unusual to receive one of these Columbian half dollars, particularly one dated 1893, in one's pocket change. The Isabella quarters, struck in 1893, were issued in much smaller quantities and therefore were not a drug on the market as the Columbian halves were.

Even though these commemoratives did not meet with great enthusiasm, the series was started, as if by accident, and the idea of selling special coins at premiums to raise money for special events took hold.

In 1900 we had our first and only commemorative dollar, the Washington Lafayette. Until this time no special denomination had been adopted for commemorative coins and they began to appear in all kinds. With the advent of the 1903 Louisiana Purchase commemorative gold dollars, we have the first of a series of gold dollars and quarter eagles. The Panama-Pacific fifty-dollar slugs, which appeared in 1915 became very rare. Coined in very limited numbers they were issued more as historical souvenirs than as coins. Even so, at the time of issue, trouble was encountered disposing of them at over face value.

People resented having to pay a premium for a coin, no matter how interesting it was or how small an issue. Little did those buyers know how greatly they would increase in value. Even in the late 1920s, dealers were more than pleased to get their capital investment out of the Panama-Pacific fifty-dollar piece plus a small premium for their efforts. I can remember the pair, both octagonal and round, being offered, uncirculated, for as little as $125 for the pair! Twenty-five dollars over face value!

While approximately a thousand of these Panama-Pacific fifty-dollar pieces were struck of each type, nearly half of them were turned in to the mint to be melted up. This leaves a little over a thousand of both in existence today.

The Panama-Pacific set—the two fifty-dollar gold pieces, a gold quarter eagle, a gold dollar, and a fifty-cent piece—created the first great urge to encourage more of this interesting series. This commemoration, having adopted so many different denominations, helped decide what future denomination was to be used—the half dollar. Since both the price and the size of the half dollar were the most popular, future commemorative coins were struck in this denomination, soon exclusively. In 1918 the Lincoln Centennial half dollar was issued, and from 1920 on, one or more different commemoratives came out every year.

Difficulty was found selling all the commemoratives that were authorized, for while the series had enlisted many ardent followers, there were not as many as there were coins. Many were available and kept the values down for a long while. Collectors were told these commemoratives were limited issues and would become valuable, but did not respond.

In 1921, the idea of making varieties that would be rarer than the regular series was first put into effect. We find the Missouri Centennial with and without star and the Grant Memorial with and without star and the two Alabamas. This was the first step toward trying to sell more coins to a limited number of buyers. As time went by, many commemorative halves were issued, some by associations which only wanted to dispose of enough coins to fill their need for funds. More enterprising concerns had the halves made for many years, from many mints, and with all kinds of minor varieties to create rarities.

The quantity of commemorative coins issued hit its peak around 1935–36. Interest at that time also hit a peak. Speculators and collectors were getting on the band wagon, buying commemoratives in quantities, making up sets, and carrying around graphs showing the fluctuations of price trends. It was not unusual for "the boys" to deal in hundreds and thousands of one issue. It was similar to stock market speculation. Some rare issues skyrocketed from $5 to $75 within a week! Such rapid profits were unheard of in the numismatic world.

As might have been expected, it couldn't last. The crash came. Overnight no one wanted to buy any commemoratives and everyone was loaded with hundreds of one kind. It took many years to get over this debacle and for holders of commemoratives to dispose of their hoards. When this finally occurred, most issues were widely distributed, and a gradual and more secure rise in values began.

The sale of new issues after 1936 was very difficult, and the government approved few. For many years the only new commemoratives struck were those under authorization from previous years, such as the Boone, Oregon Trail, Texas, and Arkansas. Very few coins were struck each year because of the sharply reduced demand and the repetition of designs. Collectors were disgusted with the "rackets" as they called them. Some hope was raised with the issue of the 1946 Iowa Centennial, for this was a new, single, and interesting coin. However, it was quickly followed by the mass of varieties of the Booker T. Washington and Washington-Carver series, the last of which, with thirty different varieties, ended in 1954.

At present the administration, on the advice of the Mint, frowns upon commemorative issues. The exploitation of many issues of the series has caused a good deal of discontent. The feeling is that the Mint is too busy to issue these special coins and that commemoratives tend to confuse the coinage of the country, creating too many designs. It is also felt that commemoratives should be issued in the form of medals. Medals, however, have never reached the popularity among collectors that coins have; the collector likes to feel his collection is of basic intrinsic value, no matter how small. The number of medals versus proof sets issued by the Mint is evidence of this.

It is too bad the situation has come to such an impasse. I feel a series of commemorative coins is educational, interesting, and can within reason be a profitable investment. The fault lies in the manner of distribution.

9.

TEDDY ROOSEVELT'S TWENTY-DOLLAR GOLD PIECE

The Smithsonian Institution received the donation by Cornelius Roosevelt, of Washington, D.C., of an experimental high-relief double eagle or twenty-dollar gold piece, dated 1907, designed by Augustus St. Gaudens at the request of President Theodore Roosevelt. This is one of the great rarities of the United States coin series and has, in addition, an unusual historical connotation since it was owned originally by Theodore Roosevelt, who devoted considerable efforts toward its design and production.

In fact, in the winter of 1905, Theodore Roosevelt met at a dinner in Washington with Augustus St. Gaudens, whose sculptures the president admired greatly. The conversation drifted to the beauty of ancient Greek coins, described by St. Gaudens as almost the only coins of real artistic merit. Why couldn't the United States have coins as beautiful as the Greek ones, the president wished to know. If St. Gaudens would model them, the president said, he would have them minted.

Thus started a unique venture in modern monetary history. Manifesting his versatility and extraordinary energy, Theodore Roosevelt found the time personally to conduct the campaign for a more artistic series of United States coinage designs. On November 6, 1905, in a letter to St. Gaudens regarding these designs, the president said:

> I want to make a suggestion. It seems to me worthwhile to try for a really good coinage; though I suppose there will be a revolt about it! I was looking at some gold coins of Alexander the Great today, and I was struck by their high relief. Would it not be well to have our coins in high relief, and also to have the rims raised? The point of having the rims raised would be, of course, to protect the figure on the coin; and if we have the figures in high relief, like the figures on the old Greek coins, they will surely last longer. What do you think of this?

For two years president and sculptor gave much time and energy to the task of producing the new coin designs. The models finally adopted for the double eagle were of unusual artistic merit. The obverse showed a standing figure of "Liberty," holding aloft in her right hand the torch of enlightenment and in her left, the olive branch of peace. On the reverse side was a rendering of a flying eagle above a rising sun.

A few experimental pieces having an extremely high relief were struck at the president's order. These exceedingly rare pieces can be easily distinguished from the ones issued later for general circulation, which also have a very high relief. The field of the rare experimental pieces is excessively concave and connects directly with the edge without any border, giving it a sharp knifelike appearance. Liberty's skirt shows two folds on the side of the right leg; the Capitol building in the background at the left is very small; and the date, 1907, is in Roman numerals. The sun, on the reverse side, has fourteen rays.

In addition to these experimental pieces, 11,250 high-relief twenty-dollar gold pieces were struck on a medal press for general distribution and may be found today in many collections. Their relief is somewhat lower than that of the experimental pieces. They have a border around the edge; Liberty's skirt has three folds on the side of the right leg; the Capitol is considerably larger; and the date, 1907, is indicated in Roman numerals. On the reverse, there are only thirteen rays extending from the sun.

For practical reasons and especially since these high-relief coins could not be struck on a regular coin press and would not stack, it was decided soon to revert to the customary flat relief. A large number of similar flat-relief double eagles were issued in 1907 (these pieces show the date in Arabic numerals) and in later years up to 1933, when the issuance of gold coins was discontinued.

Theodore Roosevelt's twenty-dollar gold piece, donated by Cornelius Roosevelt, is placed on permanent display in the Smithsonian Institution's hall of monetary history. It should remind us of Roosevelt's words about this piece: "Certain things were done, of which the economic bearing was more remote but which bore directly upon our welfare, because they add to the beauty of living and therefore to the joy of life."

10.

AMERICA'S FIRST COLONIAL COINS

The first New England coins, crude silver pieces with a simple design "NE" on the obverse, "XII" on the reverse, were the first coins struck in the Colonies. Shortage of change and the inability to get relief from the mother country prompted the Massachusetts Colony to embark upon this coining adventure to alleviate this shortage in New England. The famous Pine Tree Shilling shown below was part of this series to be struck by John Hull, who was appointed Mint Master.

After several years, when the coining operations were brought to the attention of King Charles of England, action was taken to prohibit any further issues.

While the majority were dated 1652, it is thought that they were coined for thirty years despite the King's disapproval. These crude and early pieces are actively sought by collectors and bring good prices today. They were coined in shillings, sixpence, three-pence and two-penny pieces.

11.

CHRISTIAN GOBRECHT'S FLYING EAGLE DOLLAR

In the year 1836 interest was revived in the coining of silver dollars, as none had been coined since 1803. With the proposed passage of a law reducing their weight, permission was granted to resume minting this denomination.

Christian Gobrecht, famed engraver, executed the dies for this beautiful coin shown here. The Liberty Seated design was submitted by Thomas Sully, famed Philadelphia artist, and the Flying Eagle on the reverse was designed by Titian Peale, son of Charles Willson Peale, famous painter.

In 1836, 1838 and 1839 limited quantities of these dollars were struck with minor varieties on a more or less experimental basis. All are very rare.

It was not until 1840 that the dollar came into its own. Robert Ball Hughes, an Anglo-American sculptor, was the designer. He closely copied the Liberty Seated design on the obverse, but changed the Eagle to a standing position on the reverse. This famous Liberty Seated design was used on dollars and smaller denominations from then until 1891.

12.

HISTORY OF THE "DOLLAR"

From the time of the Roman Empire, and through the Dark Ages the predominant size of silver coins was copied after the Ancient Roman Denarius, about the size of our present day dime. Times were pretty lean and silver pieces were consequently few and far between.

In the year 1516 a rich silver mine was discovered in Joachim's dale, a mining district in Bohemia. The count of Schlitz, by whom it was appropriated, struck a great number of large silver coins. The first had the date 1518 and the effigy of St. Joachim upon it. These were to be of the same value in silver as the many gold *gulden* then in use in trade. This Joachimsthaler has the distinction of being known as the first "Thaler" or silver coin of approximately one ounce in weight and around the size of our silver dollars.

From that time on the "thaler" became one of the most popular coins in Europe. Most countries and German states issued hundreds of varieties of these. The French issued coins of similar size "Ecus", the English their "Crowns", the Spanish their "Pieces of 8" (8 Reals). The name of such coins in other countries were changed to "Daler", "Dalar", "Daalder", "Tallero".

In the Western Hemisphere the Spanish "Pieces of 8" circulated widely during Colonial days. The British kept as much English Specie as possible from the American Colonies, creating serious shortages here. They also prohibited the coinage of coins. It is therefore not surprising the Spanish 8 Real coins soon became the principal medium to circulate and soon became known as the "Spanish Milled Dollar".

It is said that the Dollar George Washington threw across the Rapahannock River was one of these and indeed it must have been for our country did not coin any silver dollars until 1794.

We sometimes wonder why we did not adopt the English Denominations when we first started coining. Pounds, shillings and pence were used in all transactions with England, the parent country, during the Colonial days. We find that early Colonial paper money was issued in English denominations but during and after the Revolution one finds the gradual change to dollars and cents, some of the earlier notes even being redeemable in "Spanish Milled Dollars". No doubt antagonism over the war with England and the use of the Spanish coins influenced our country to adopt the dollar and cents denominations.

Our silver dollar has had a stormy path. From 1794 through 1803 they were coined in varying quantities. From 1803 through 1840 we have a gap of thirty-seven years when none were coined for circulation. It seems the amount of silver contained in the early dollars was too great. In 1837 Congress passed a law providing that 3½ grains of the alloy be extracted from the authorized weight of the dollar which at that time weighed 416 grains. This made the new dollar weight 412½ grains. The only dollars struck between 1803 and 1840 were the 1804s of questionable authenticity, and the rare pattern or experimental pieces of 1836, 1838 and 1839, forerunners of the regular issued Liberty Seated dollars of 1840.

Standard silver dollars were again suspended with the issue of Trade dollars in 1873, designed to capture trade in the Orient. As these were not successful they were terminated in 1878 and standard silver dollars were again coined from then on until 1904. The few Trade dollars that were issued between 1879 and 1885 were struck for collectors only. In 1904 all dollars were discontinued due to the lack of bullion.

The Peace dollar first made its appearance in 1921, seventeen years later, and was coined continuously from then until 1935, the last year silver dollars were struck.

13.
ONE OF THE WORLD'S FIRST COMMEMORATIVE COINS

John George I, Elector of Saxony, had this "thaler" struck in order to commemorate the hundredth anniversary of the "Confession of Augsberg", the important Protestant statement drawn up by Martin Luther at the Reformation and presented to Emperor Charles V on June 25, 1530. On one side we see John, Elector of Saxony, in 1530 facing right with sword, and the date June 25, 1530; on the other, Elector John George I facing right with sword, and the date June 25, 1630, one hundred years later.

This is without doubt one of the earliest commemorative coins known and is an excellent example of a "thaler," the original denomination from which our "dollar" came.

14.

HOW TO DETERMINE WHETHER A COIN IS UNCIRCULATED

I cannot stress enough the importance of accurate classification on condition in coins. If one becomes a coin collector, this exacting work should be the first to be mastered. A good amount of money can be lost by paying high prices for coins or coin collections that have been grossly overrated. If, when buying coins, there is any doubt in your mind as to whether a certain piece is in the condition represented, take it to an expert or another experienced collector. He will gladly give you an opinion free of charge. When purchasing a large collection, don't hesitate to have a dealer appraise it for you and give you his written expert opinion. It may cost you a fee for an expert appraisal, but this sum may save you many hundreds in the long run. Dealers KNOW what to look for.

With the steadily increasing values of uncirculated coins, it is essential that the serious collector know how to determine whether or not a coin is really uncirculated. Because of some of the cleaning processes used today, very careful scrutiny is necessary. I do not mean a cleaned coin cannot be considered uncirculated; what I mean is that many cleaned coins look like uncirculated pieces when closer scrutiny shows they have some wear.

It must be remembered that truly uncirculated pieces, if properly cleaned, are not decreased in value, even though under some circumstances it is preferable to have uncirculated pieces in their natural state. Too frequently, we look at a coin and, because it appears bright and new, consider it uncirculated, when the actual wear upon such a piece should be the determining factor.

I shall try to describe what I have found to be the first spots to wear on a coin, the first places to look for wear on what appears to be an uncirculated coin. I shall also mention other telltale defects to watch for.

Lincoln cents show their first wear on the cheekbone of Lincoln's bust. In the twenties, for a few years, Lincoln cents were struck very poorly so the coinage appears blurred, and these would be exceptions to the rule. Such blurred coins, even though uncirculated, would not be considered choice uncirculated coins.

Indian Heads first show wear on the obverse at the lock of hair at the lower right-hand bottom part of the bust. The ribbon hanging down is next to show wear. On the reverse, the highlights of the bow at the bottom of the wreath first wear.

The tip of the headdress above the word "Liberty" first shows wear on a large cent back to 1840. Prior to that date, the hairlock below the headdress, the eyebrow, and the cheek give telltale evidence. On the reverse, the highlighted leaves in the wreaths must be watched for wear. These coins are rather well struck. They should also be watched for minute scratches on the field of the obverse and reverse, on the head, and most important of all, on the edges of the coin. I have seen large cents that appear to have no wear at all, but close examination shows they contain many tiny scratches and nicks which immediately remove them from the uncirculated category.

Color plays a vitally important part in the valuation of large cents. Rich browns and steel color are the most desirable. Partially red, red, and brilliant are less desirable because they are apt to corrode under certain conditions.

The earlier large cents are a study for an expert. Being crudely struck and with so many varieties, it is difficult to name any specific places of where to look for wear. Each coin must be examined with the greatest care. Look for minute tiny scratches. Examine the color of the coin and its glossy surface. Should one of these "seem" to be worn slightly, it might well be the manner in which it was struck.

The most desirable condition for an early large cent is one with a rich dark brown, glossy surface, well centered, evenly struck, with no apparent signs of wear, corrosion, tiny nicks, scratches, and the like. Large cents in this condition are very valuable and should be carefully handled to maintain their status.

The description of wear for large cents covers that of the half-cent series.

The Eagle cents of 1856 through 1858 first show signs of wear upon the eagle's breast directly below the wing. The wing tip and eyebrow should also be examined. Some Eagle cents exist with very smooth tail feathers. This does not indicate wear, however, for many were lightly struck there.

Two-cent pieces are easy to detect for the "we" of the motto is the first item to go. Blurred horizontal lines in the shield are frequent, but these are not necessarily signs of wear, for many were coined in this manner.

The lock of hair above the ear first shows signs of wear on the three-cent nickel piece. These should also be closely examined for color, for soiled or discolored pieces are not desirable. Mint bloom should be evident upon these.

The Jefferson nickel wears first on Jefferson's cheekbone. On the reverse, just below the dome of Monticello, first signs of wear can be detected by a slight dulling or discoloration from the original glossy uncirculated look of the rest of the coin. These may be cleaned, but it is very difficult to erase this dulling effect.

Buffalo nickels are about the most difficult to identify in uncirculated condition. First, examine them for their original glossy mint bloom or color. If this is satisfactory, then examine the sharp edges of the coins for slight telltale hairlike scratches that will indicate circulation.

After this, closely examine the shoulder of the buffalo which will appear worn, for Buffalo nickels were coined in this manner, but examine the smooth shoulder for more telltale hairlike scratches. His hip, tail tip, and horn should be sharp. Next examine the cheek and just above the braid on the Indian's head for the same hairlike scratches. If the coin has no wear, no hairlike scratches on the above spots, and has its original mint bloom, you can assume it is a truly uncirculated coin.

The Liberty nickel first shows wear on the lock of hair over the temple and on the reverse highlights of the leaves in the wreath. The majority of Liberty nickels were struck very sharp, but blurred coinage is known in the years of 1911 and 1912.

Slight dulling of the original mint bloom on the highlights is the first sign of wear, as was the case with the Jefferson nickel.

The tiny crosslike emblem atop the shield of the Shield nickel shows evidence of wear first. On the reverse, examine the "5" for minute, hairlike scratches and signs of wear.

A great many of the three-cent silver pieces were not struck very sharply. Of the first design, these should have mint bloom and lack light hairlike scratches. The type II three-cent piece, from 1854 on, has sharply defined lines around the star. These are the first spots to wear although these tiny coins usually wear fairly evenly all over.

The first signs of wear on Liberty-Seated coins, whether they are half dimes, dimes, quarters, halves, or silver dollars, appear on the ear of the head (some are known to have been struck blurred, however), then on the thigh of Liberty Seated. The ribbon below the wreath, on the reverse of the dime and half dime, wears first. Quarters and halves first show wear on the eyebrow and upper beak of the eagle, then on the upper wing tips.

Bust-type quarters and halves wear first on the lock of hair near the ear, next on the clasp on the ribbon at the lower part of the bust. On the reverse, the eagle's upper bill and the top edges of the wings wear first. Some of these coins are known to have been lightly struck so the general appearance of the rest of the coin must be taken into consideration.

Telltale signs of wear first show up on the eagle's wing, right in the center of the coin, on a Peace dollar. On a Morgan dollar wear appears first on the eagle's breast and head. With both of these coins, the reverse seems to show wear a good deal faster than the obverse.

Barber quarters, halves, and dimes wear first on the obverse on the lock of hair over the forehead and temple directly below the word "Liberty." The cheek next shows discoloration and dulling. The reverse of the quarters and halves wears first directly above the eye of the eagle and the claws in his left talon.

The Liberty-Walking half-dollar coins first show wear on the breast of the eagle on the reverse. The head, breasts, and left leg of Miss Liberty are the next telltale signs. Franklin half dollars show their first sign of wear right in the center of the bell and on the cheek of Franklin. A slight dullness is the very first sign of wear.

Liberty-Standing quarters first show signs of wear on the knee of Miss Liberty. A slight flattening appears as the first telltale sign of wear. A number of these quarters were coined with flat heads, which appear worn, but this does not necessarily mean the coin is not uncirculated. Watch that knee for the first real signs of wear. On the reverse, the eagle's breast wears first, but not nearly as soon as the knee on the obverse. I have seen many beautiful (cleaned) Liberty-Standing quarters with full head, but with that telltale sign of wear on the knee. Don't be fooled by this one! Washington quarters first wear on the eagle's breast.

Now consider our early types of silver dollars. The type with flowing hair wears first on the eagle's breast and on the lock of hair directly behind the ear. The bust type, small eagle, on the reverse shows wear on the eagle's breast, on the obverse on the draped bust, directly above the first two digits of the date and to the extreme right bottom. The cheek wears next.

On Liberty Seated silver dollars, the first wear shows on the right thigh, closely followed by the forehead and the word "Liberty" on the shield; on the reverse, the eagle's beak and upper tips of wings wear first. On trade dollars, the knee, left breast, and head on the obverse show the first signs of wear; on the reverse the eagle's left leg, then upper tips of wings.

Commemorative coins should be examined carefully as many show wear, particularly in the early series. The first spots to wear are listed below:

Columbian Half Dollars

Obverse: cheek and center lock of hair

Reverse: center sail of ship; next, center of globes

New Rochelle, New York, 300th Anniversary

Obverse: the calf's hip

Reverse: highlights of the fleur-de-lis

Iowa Centennial

Obverse: the eagle's breast

Reverse: center columns, building, and the tower

Booker T. Washington Memorial

Obverse: cheek and nose

Reverse: highlights of center letters

Washington-Carver
Obverse: the prominent cheek
Reverse: the whole map of the United States
Isabella Quarter
Obverse: cheek
Reverse: head and left forearm
Lafayette Dollar
Obverse: cheek of Washington
Reverse: leg of equestrian; next, head
Panama-Pacific Exposition (1915)
Obverse: head and left arm
Reverse: eagle's breast
Lincoln, Illinois, Centennial
Obverse: cheekbone
Reverse: eagle's breast directly below forward part of left wing
Maine Centennial
Obverse: fingers of left figure on scythe
Reverse: ribbon holding wreath at bottom
Pilgrim Tercentenary
Obverse: cheek, hatbrim, and book tip
Reverse: high side of ship
Missouri Centennial
Obverse: cheek and side of hat
Reverse: pioneer's arm, both heads
Alabama Centennial
Obverse: Kilby's cheek and forehead
Reverse: eagle's breast directly above left leg
Grant Memorial
Obverse: hair at temple
Reverse: leaves of trees
Monroe Centennial
Obverse: cheek and hair over temple
Reverse: the faint figures in the maps of North and South America; examine coin for light hairlike scratches (This is a lightly struck coin hard to tell when slightly used.)
Huguenot-Walloon Tercentenary
Obverse: outstanding rim and top of hat, also cape
Reverse: hull of ship and shrouds

Lexington-Concord Sesquicentennial
Obverse: fingers holding the gun
Reverse: point of block house at center

15.

PROOF COINS MUST BE PERFECT

Proof coins are described by most publications as "Coins specially struck with mirror-like surface, for collectors, at Philadelphia only. Also sandblast and mat proof." But there is a lot more to them than that.

Today, they are very carefully struck to insure perfect specimens. Until recently, they were struck by hand to insure perfection. At all times, the dies used were polished, as were the planchets. This gave the coins their mirror-like finish.

A genuine proof must be perfect. Its field, including the tiny spaces between letters and designs, must have this mirror-like finish. The highlights of the coin are sharp and have a "frosted" or "uncirculated" look, causing the designs to "stand out" from their mirror-like background. The edges are usually sharp and the coin is perfectly centered.

Proof coins are truly beautiful coins, whether they are of gold, silver, or copper. Sandblast or mat proofs have all the above qualifications, with the exception of the mirror-like finish; they have a dull velvety-type surface instead.

While the first regularly recognized issue of proofs for collectors commenced in 1858, proofs were coined before that time. The first early proofs were trial or experimental pieces to test designs and dies. Very few were struck and consequently they are very rare. These were usually not offered for sale to collectors but were more "presentation" pieces, samples of coinage, and so forth.

In 1858, when proofs were first offered for sale to collectors, the number struck was very small. Records of how many proofs were coined prior to 1877 are spotty, but from what information we have we can tell that the quantities were very small. By examining the records one can see how the interest in proof coins steadily increased as the years went by, popularity centering on the lower denominations.

During the nineteenth century, proof sets were offered as minor sets, complete sets, and those with gold. The minor sets were by far the most popular, the complete sets following second in popularity. Gold coins were not very popular in proof even though their premium cost was very little over the face value. Probably, this was due to the initial face-value investment involved. The coinage of proof double eagles ranged from only 20 to 158 proofs per year from 1865 to 1907.

Proofs were discontinued in 1915 and were not resumed again until 1936. The maximum number of proofs struck in 1915 for any denomination was around 1,000. The number struck in 1936 that can make up proof sets was around 3,300. This was quite an increase, but nothing like what occurred from 1936 to 1957 when 1,000,000 or so proof sets were coined.

From 1936 through 1942, proofs were not sold as "sets" only, as they are today. One could purchase any quantity of any denomination; you had to make up your own sets. From 1950 on, proofs have been sold as sets only.

Many "early strikes" of regular issue coins appear to be proofs, for the new dies frequently give the coins a mirror-like surface. This is often true with branch mint coins, but it must be remembered that no proofs were ever struck at any of the branch mints. While it is very difficult to detect these, it will be found that they never have the sharp, well struck edges of a genuine proof. The highlights are usually not sharp and the coin is not perfectly centered.

One frequently comes across attempts to fake proofs. Buffing will give an uncirculated coin a mirror-like finish, but this usually can be detected because the mirror-like finish is on the designs as well as the field. Even coins done more carefully, so that the designs are not buffed, can be detected by examining the tiny surfaces between the letters and designs where a buffer cannot get. Of course the sharp edges of such coins are lacking also.

Uncirculated coins that most frequently look like proof coins when they are not are: silver dollars, 1878 up, from all mints; Liberty-Seated halves, prior to 1890; quarters, prior to 1890; a few dimes in the 1870s; the 1866 nickel; the 1865 three-cent piece; gold dollars, particularly in the 1880s; and some of the later three-dollar gold pieces. With regard to the gold two-and-one-half-, five-, ten-, and twenty-dollar pieces, these sometimes are found with proof-like luster but are usually somewhat scratched, indicating contact with other coins.

Several of the scarcer, shorter issues, such as the four-dollar Stellas; the three-dollar coins of 1873, 1875, and 1876; the twenty-cent pieces of 1877 and 1878; the nickel three-cent pieces of 1877 and 1878; and the two-cent pieces of 1873, were only struck in proof, even though used specimens or "debased" proofs are occasionally found of these coins.

The three-dollar series, the nickel three-cent pieces, and the two-cent pieces were coins purely for collectors, to maintain a "consecutive run of dates." The 1873 two-cent pieces and the 1877 and 1878 twenty-cent pieces struck for this reason turned out to be the last of the series.

The four-dollar Stellas were really trial or experimental pieces and were never coined for actual use.

Some denominations during the 1880s became unpopular for regular use but were coined for a decade or so in small quantities, probably to satisfy the collectors' demand for a complete "run of dates."

16.

BEWARE OF COUNTERFEITS

The rapid price rise of nearly all United States coins has created a flood of counterfeits, altered dates, and other kinds of forgeries, many of which are so clever that the best experts are sometimes fooled. Below are those to watch out for:

Twenty-dollar gold pieces. All twenties are being coined, of the proper amount of gold, in foreign countries, designed to be sold to American collectors. They can be detected by examining the feathers in the center of the eagle on the reverse. These feathers are too sharply tooled. They also have a very proof-like, mirror-type surface. Beware of Liberty-Head types of rare dates, Philadelphia Mint, for the common branch mint coins are having the mint marks cleverly removed. Foreign made counterfeit Liberty Heads have very sharp milling—appear too new.

Ten-dollar gold pieces. Watch the 1858*P*; these are known to exist with their mint marks removed (branch mint). All tens are being coined in Europe at present.

Five-dollar gold pieces. Watch the 1909*O* as the *O* mint mark is known to have been added. All fives are being counterfeited.

Three-dollar gold pieces. There is a possibility that the later dates are being struck in Europe. They have a mirror-like appearance.

Four-dollar Stellas. Beware of gold-plated patterns struck in inferior metals and being sold as gold Stellas. The 1880 series coins are being struck presently in Europe.

Quarter eagles ($2.50). Both types, Indian Head and Liberty Head, are being struck in large quantities in Europe. They have the correct weight in gold and are very nearly perfect.

On fake Liberty Heads the head is too sharp, the edge of the coin is a trifle flat, and the milling is too sharp. These have a granular surface and they come in many dates. As to the Indian Heads, it is difficult to tell, but there again the milling is too fine and sharp.

Gold dollars. Coins of pretty nearly every date and mint have been copied. These, for the most part, have a granular surface, the beading on the edge tends to be too flat, the milling much too sharp, the deep-cut word "Liberty" on the headdress is usually sharp in the center and weak toward the end of each word. These are the new counterfeits struck in Europe and are very dangerous, being of the correct weight and fineness of gold. Old counterfeits are very easy to detect, for the gold content is inferior. The very rare 1854*C* has been faked by adding a sweated letter *C* to it; I have seen two of these in the last six months. Mint marks also are known to have been sweated to nearly all of the rarer branch mint gold dollars. In all denominations, these new European gold counterfeits are made by the centrifugal molding process and are very cleverly done.

Silver dollars. Removing the mint mark from an 1895*O* or *S* is done to make it the rare 1895*P* dollar. This coin was only struck in proof and, to be genuine, should be a perfect proof.

Half dollars. There are no outstanding new forgeries of halves recently other than the well-known addition of a star to the Grant Memorial half dollar. This is easily detected because the Grant stars were coined first. When the star was removed from the dies, a few minor defects were also corrected, namely slight bulges at the neck and below the nose. These always appear on the genuine Grant stars and never on the Grant without star. Counterfeit Grant stars also, at times, have a flattened spot on the reverse.

Quarter dollars. The 1923*S*, being rare, is being made by changing the 8 on a 1928*S* to a 3. Also, the mint mark on a 1913*D* is being retooled to look like an *S*. 1932 with a *"D"* cleverly added.

Dimes. Beware of the 1916*D*! I have seen these altered in all conditions; recently I saw a "good" one altered from a 1919*D*. Many have been faked by sweating a *D* cleverly on to a 1916*P*. These can be detected under a 20-power glass; close examination of the *D* will show some slight discoloration around the initial. Very frequently, the initial is out of its correct position. If sweated on, close examination will show indications of the base of the *D* tending to "round in" where it is attached to the coin, rather than being part of the planchet. A dealer recently had a roll of 1916*D* Unc. dimes offered to him. He picked the false "*D*s" off of the coins and sent all back to the seller!

Another clever fraud is to take two dimes, a 1916*P* and a 1917*D* and mount them, with the 1916*P* obverse showing and the 1917*D* reverse showing, in an expensive plastic holder. In still another dangerous fraud, they punch the metal on the obverse out a little and fill it in so it is hardly noticeable; then with the bulge on the reverse they create a *D*. Very cleverly done! The celebrated 1894*S* has had *S* sweated on to the Philadelphia coin. I have not seen one of these, however, in thirty years.

Nickels. Watch 1950*D*. They are now cutting the tail off of 1959*D* to make it look like 1950*D*. Watch your 1937*D* three-legged nickels; they are now grinding off the one leg. To detect a genuine three-legged nickel, the point under the belly of the buffalo is long and very sharp; this does not appear on any other Buffalo nickel.

Watch this new angle. Dates are being put on dateless nickels by applying acids. The 1913 Liberty Head has for years been altered, either from a 1903 or a 1910. The 1895 nickels are being altered to 1885.

From 1866 through 1873 we had both the silver five-cent pieces of half dimes and the nickel five-cent pieces, two different types of this denomination. To top that off, the first Liberty nickels of 1883 did not have the word *cents* on them. After being gold-plated, they were frequently passed as five-dollar gold pieces, being the same size.

The twenty-cent coins were so similar to quarters that these two were frequently mistaken for each other. Last, but not least, a two-and-one-half-dollar gold piece is the same size as a cent. Many have been passed as cents, in error, due to this similarity.

I guess the five definitely different denominations we have today are the best.

Cents. This is the most popular series. The *D* is cleverly being ground off of the 1960 cents to make them *P*, small date only. 1937*S* cents are being retooled to look like 1931*S*. The 1922*D* cents are being changed to 1922 plain cents.

The 1914*D* is being made from an altered 1944*D*, with the first 4 being changed to a 1. The *D* is being sweated on the 1914*P* and the field is being ground down so that only the metal for the *D* is left. These are the hardest to identify, because one must examine the field around the letter to detect the concave depression. On 1909*S-VDB*, the letter *S* is being sweated to a common 1909*VDB*. (Initials of Victor D. Brenner, the coin's designer.) Indian cents apparently have not been tampered with. But watch the 1856 Eagle cent. These are commonly altered from an 1858.

Watch your coins; any coins valued at from a few dollars up are liable to be forged.

Be very careful of early rarities, particularly in Colonials, large cents and half cents; some of the electrotypes are so realistic they fool many an expert. An electrotype is a copper-plated lead piece made as an exact copy of the original rare coin. Electrotypes are considered by the government to be counterfeits if they are made in imitation of regular United States coinages. I know of an antique dealer who payed $110 for an electrotype of the rare 1792 Washington Large-Eagle half dollar, not knowing that it was a fake. A customer of ours recently purchased a collection of half cents from another collector for a high price, only to find that the 1796, 1831, 1852 cents—all very rare dates—were electrotypes. Those three coins, if genuine, would have been worth the major cost of the collection.

How can you detect electrotypes? Sometimes it is easy, other times not. First, an electrotype never has any lettering or milling on the edges; at least, I have never seen one that did. Second, sometimes one can detect a fine crack in the middle of the edge running around the coin where the two copper coatings have been pressed together; sometimes this has been eliminated by careful smoothing off of the edges. In any event, one can usually see one or the other: a slight crack or evidence of light smoothing on the edges of the coin. Third, usually an electrotype does not ring true. Its ring is sometimes remarkably near that of an original coin, however, in that the old copper coins do not ring very much anyway. Fourth, unless an electrotype has been very heavily plated, it usually can be bent with the fingers because the lead inside is soft. The antiquated system of biting a coin to test its genuineness may work if the plating is not too thick. Fifth, scraping the edge with a sharp knife usually will expose the lead under the thin copper plating; however, some electrotypes are so heavily plated that to scrape through seriously damages the coin if it turns out to be genuine. This is all I can suggest concerning electrotype detection, and I repeat, electrotypes are found mostly of early American Colonials, large cents.

17.
MINT ERRORS AND THE RATING SCALE

Coins that are off-center or that have something wrong with them, formerly known as freaks, have now been given the name of *mint errors*. In the manufacture of coins, the mint carefully checks the new coins as they are coined, but occasionally a misstamped coin, or bill for that matter, manages to escape the eyes of the checkers and get into circulation. A good many of these mint errors are unique; others are quite common due to the ease with which certain errors occur and are overlooked. There is an association for mint-error collectors.

The difficulty of describing mint errors prompted the rating scale, which makes it easier to understand what the error is. For instance, on off-center coins, the clock is used as a guide. If you place the coin in front of you, the top would be numeral 12, and the circle of the coin would be divided into twelve equal spaces like the face of a clock. Thus, if you have an off-center Lincoln cent and the design is off to the right at about the number 3 of the clock, it is known as a "3 o'clock" off-center coin. If the coin is off at the bottom of the planchet, it is "6 o'clock" and so on around the face of the clock.

Degrees of off-center are figured in fractions of an inch. If the design is halfway off, showing half the planchet blank, and to the right, as described above in the first example, it is "3, ½ off." If the degree off is one quarter, showing three quarters of the coin design and one-fourth blank, it is known as "3, ¼ off." Therefore, the professional description of the last coin is: Lincoln cent 1911*P* ¼ O.C. in 3 o'clock.

Coins slightly off-center, or eclipsed (a circular piece out of the edge of the planchet at some spot), are the most common mint errors. This does not mean that all are, however. I recently had a large cent with the rare date 1811 in almost uncirculated condition which was off-center about ⅛ at 2 on the obverse. The unusual thing about this cent was that, while it was the same amount off on the reverse, the design was *incused*, or cut in, rather than raised up and very sharp. This most likely was the result of two planchets being struck at once and the design of one cent being impressed in reverse on the other. The combination of errors, plus the rarity of the coin and its condition, make it very rare.

A popular type of mint error is the cent that is struck on a silver planchet. This can happen when a dime planchet gets mixed up with the cent ones; consequently the cent design is struck on the silver dime planchet. Many persons think these are very rare, but there are more of them than one realizes. A count made recently indicated that there were approximately forty-five known silver cents. They are frequently quoted as being worth thousands of dollars, but auction records indicate a bonafide sale of one of these at $700. Most dealers shy from this coin.

One of the most sought after and popular mint errors is the copper cent of 1943, the year they made steel cents only. Many people claim to have these copper cents, but close inspection shows that nearly all are fakes. It is very easy to copper-plate a steel cent, but this can be detected by giving it a magnet test. If the cent adheres to the magnet, you may be certain there is a steel cent under the plating.

Errors in paper money are also ardently sought. The commonest errors are bills that are slightly off-center. Also common are bills that had the paper folded slightly so that there is a "white spot" across some part of the note. Probably the most desirable are notes that have one denomination on one side, and another on the other. I recently saw one of these on exhibition, a one dollar reverse and a five dollar obverse.

Other very unusual mint errors are bills with composite folds that give a white, unprinted, accordion effect; notes printed heavily on one side of the reverse or obverse with ink fading to nothing on the other side; and notes with signatures and numbers upside down. All these are very rare. And one must remember that mint errors, as well as all coins, must be in perfect condition to demand the best prices. Even though the error is an unusual one, if the note has been used a lot, its value is one-tenth what it would have been had it been crisp-new.

18.
SHALL I CLEAN MY COINS?

This age-old question has been bothering collectors and dealers for a long time. Originally, the cleaning of coins was taboo and those that first attempted cleaning did their best to have the coins they cleaned look as much as possible as if they had not been cleaned. Today, well-cleaned coins are accepted as readily as (and sometimes more readily than) those that have been kept in their original state, with exceptions. The coins cleaned and the cleaner used determine the desirability of the coin in question.

Never clean a badly worn coin of any kind. In the first place, it is a waste of time and, cleaning a coin that is in a condition inferior to very fine will never enhance it.

PROOFS

Proofs in gold seldom if ever will need cleaning. In silver they frequently become tarnished and are preferred so by collectors. If the tarnish is not too dark, Silver Dip purchased in your local supermarket will brighten them without scratching. Don't leave the coin in the dip more than five seconds or so, and rinse immediately with water. Dry with a soft cleansing tissue. Proof nickels will react favorably to the foregoing treatment.

For bronze and copper coins, leave proofs alone. A nicely toned proof cent is more desirable than one that is brilliantly cleaned. If there are specks or corrosion spots on the coin, it will then have to be cleaned, but it is questionable whether the spots will come off and, if they do, whether the cleaning will not harm the proof surface. Silver proofs that have been cleaned seem to be more desirable to the collector than uncleaned ones because detection is difficult and they like their proofs bright in silver. In copper, however, toned ones are more desirable, for the brightness of a cleaned copper coin is easily detected.

UNCIRCULATED COINS

Gold uncirculated coins rarely need cleaning. At times it might be advisable to wash them gently with Ivory soap and warm water. Silver coins, if lightly tarnished, can be brightened nicely by using Silver Dip as suggested for the proofs (a five-second dip and then a quick rinse). If heavily tarnished, silver coins should be cleaned as follows: make a paste of bicarbonate of soda and water. Do not use the ordinary inexpensive brand of soda available in grocery stores, but use the better grade found in drugstores; the texture of the cheaper brand is coarse and may scratch, whereas the better brand is smoother and does not tend to scratch as much. Be certain your fingers are soft and smooth with no nicks or scratches on the skin. It is a good idea to soak them a minute or so in warm water to soften. Then rub the coin gently with the paste until all tarnish is gone. Don't forget the edges.

COPPER COINS

Large cents or half cents in copper should never be cleaned. Indian Heads and Lincolns should not be cleaned if they are naturally brilliant or red. If they are toned down so that only a slight amount of red or no red shows, it probably is better to clean them today than leave them as they are, for a dark uncirculated cent of the small size does not seem to be as desirable as a cleaned brilliant one. A product called Care can be used on copper and bronze coins. This does not change their color but removes grease and dirt and gives them a glossy protective coating. Brilliantize does a good job even removing spots, provided one follows instructions. The cent will be very bright when finished and really nice looking, far superior to what it formerly looked like. Specks and spots can also be removed if they are on the coin. There is a tendency for copper coins to tone down more rapidly after cleaning than they would naturally, and this should be kept in mind.

VERY FINE AND EXTREMELY FINE COINS

Gold rarely needs cleaning. Ivory soap and warm water should do, if it is absolutely necessary. Silver pieces can be cleaned with bicarbonate of soda following the instructions given for uncirculated silver pieces. This usually improves the looks of the coin. Copper or bronze coins in this condition should never be cleaned. They look better in their natural state.

Silver will tarnish very quickly, particularly if exposed to air and other chemicals that affect it. It is difficult to believe that brilliant uncirculated or proof coins as old as a hundred or more years could possibly have lasted all that while without ever having been tarnished. It is my opinion that nearly all choice silver coins have been cleaned at some time or other and perhaps many times. It hasn't hurt them; in fact, had tarnish been allowed to increase, the coin would finally have become black and the tarnish would have had a permanently bad effect on the condition of the coin. The surface of very badly tarnished silver coins begins to be eaten away and can never be brought back, the corrosive quality of the tarnish having deteriorated the value of the coin.

Many collectors of large cents prefer their uncirculated specimens in a rich brown or steel color that is acquired naturally through the years. The film that gives these cents this fine glossy surface is a protection preventing the annoying corrosion spots that so frequently appear on cents that are red or brilliant. This is not the case with collectors of small cents; with this series they want them brilliant or red even though these, too, are subject to the same annoying spots. I wonder when small-cent collectors will follow the large-cent collectors and will appreciate the value of rich, colored small cents, rather than the brilliant ones that are subject to deterioration.

19.

HOW TO SELL A COIN COLLECTION

For some time I have wanted to write about the sale of coins, how to go about it and how to get what they are worth. A reader of mine wanted to know what a widow should do to sell a coin collection. This is a very difficult problem for an inexperienced person.

How to go about selling a collection depends upon the value of the collection. If it is a matter of a few hundred dollars, an outright sale is the best. If it is a collection running in excess of several thousand dollars, the story is entirely different.

In the first place, every collector should make arrangements for the sale of his collection while he is still collecting. Since he has dealt (and is dealing) with many large dealers he is in a good position to form an opinion as to whom he would trust his collection with and whom he would not. This information should be passed on to his heirs. The sale of a collection of size has to depend upon the absolute trust in the dealer purchasing it or handling its sale. There are many honest dealers in this country, but there are a few others who will use all kinds of slick tricks to get the most for the least amount of money.

When death occurs, the first step is that the collection will have to be appraised for both state and federal inheritance taxes. Appraisals can be done on both a low wholesale or a high retail valuation. Expert appraisers should give both the wholesale and retail valuation. For inheritance tax purposes, a figure between the two should be used.

It is advisable not to keep the appraisal valuations too low for this purpose, because when the collection is sold there would then be a much higher capital gains tax which would cost more than paying a higher inheritance tax.

The choice of an appraiser is very important. Get the best and to your knowledge the most honest.. Pay his fee rather than accept a free appraisal. This keeps you from being obligated to any one person in the event of sale and should get you a better appraisal. There is a great temptation for appraisers to keep values down low on a free appraisal with an eye to purchasing the collection. An appraiser should be a disinterested party, not the prospective purchaser of the collection or his agent.

Next we come to the manner of selling, whether it is outright for cash or at auction. If sold outright, one should expect to receive between 50 and 70 percent of the retail sales value. This does not mean the guide book or catalog value, but the amount the coins would actually sell for. This will vary considerably from guide book prices depending upon what the collection contains.

Proofs and key rarities usually retail for as much as full guide book prices, and in many instances for considerably above these valuations. Extreme rarities in great demand can go at two, three, and even ten times catalog value. Circulated coins of the more common variety, even ordinary uncirculated coins, rarely sell up to guide book valuations; usually they sell at from 20 to 40 percent under them.

The discount paid from retail values of 50 to 70 percent depends upon the type of material the collection contains and the amount of work involved in selling the material. One must always remember that a dealer is in business to earn his living and is entitled to his profits for his efforts.

Now we come to selling at auction. This is the manner in which all of the leading collections are sold. It has advantages and disadvantages. While cash advances on a consignment can usually be gotten, the final settlement is usually slower than a cash sale because of the length of time it takes to handle the sale. The advantages are first that the auctioneer is very anxious to realize as much as possible for the collection. The more he can realize, the more his commission will be. He will catalog the coins to their best advantage, and hidden or unknown rarities that otherwise might not be mentioned in an outright sale will be featured in order to get the most for the collection.

Surprises also occur which even conscientious dealers might not expect when purchasing outright. A coin which a dealer would normally purchase for full guide book price, suspecting it would sell for considerably more, sold recently at auction for three times guide book price!

Other advantages of the auction method include a complete published and printed record in the catalog of the collection. Also a complete printed and priced list is made of what the collection brought for every lot. And lastly, when desired, the name of the collector is published in conjunction with the sale of the collection, crediting him for his efforts in compiling it.

The auction method does take time. It will take the cataloger about a month to prepare the catalog. A month should be allowed to let the printer print it and get it into the mail. Then four to six weeks should be allowed for the collectors and dealers to send in their bids. At the termination of the sale, another month should be allowed for payments to come on the lots sold. So one can expect to have settlement in full thirty days after the termination of the auction sale. Insofar as one must wait six months for appraisal for inheritance tax purposes in order to have the profit from the sale come under capital gains rather than income tax, the length of time the auction method takes is no disadvantage.

The fee an auctioneer gets for his service ranges between 10 and 25 percent of the prices realized and should include all costs, insurance, advertising, printing, etc.

Inexperienced people sometimes fear the auction method, being afraid the coins will go for a price way below value. This is not the case. Auctioneers who run large, nationwide sales cover the market so completely, both as to dealers and collectors, there is little opportunity for any lot to go for a ridiculous price. Sometimes an unpopular item sells at a price that appears to be quite cheap, but that is really what it is worth.

The best auctions are those run by dealers who have specialized in this selling method for many years, for in so doing they have built up a clientele and a reputation that encourages good bidding. The best sales are a combination of mail bids and then a public sale commenced with the high mail bid. This system brings the best prices, encourages competition, and the prices realized are publicly announced.

WATCH OUT FOR THE FOLLOWING WHEN SELLING FOR CASH:

Downgrading. Downgrading is listing or grading a coin as inferior to what it actually is. I know of a collection of beautiful proofs that was purchased several years ago as "uncirculated" by an unscrupulous dealer.

Disinterest. A common practice among "slickys" is to push the choice pieces aside, concentrate on a few common ones, pay a good price for these, and get the real rare coins for a song.

Use of fear. Many a gold coin has been purchased, under threat of penalty to own (a law which is nonexistent), at as low as half face value.

Omission. Lots of rare coins have been sold for a song simply by the purchaser forgetting to mention that they are rare and buying a group as a "lot."

WATCH OUT FOR THE FOLLOWING WHEN SELLING AT AUCTION:

High cash advances, too-low commission charges. High cash advances and too-low commission charges are inducements that are likely to work to your disadvantage. They are come-ons to get your coins.

Local club auctions. These are honest sales but they do not have the number of bidders necessary to bring good prices. They are usually started with a minimum bid which causes a good percentage of the items to be returned unsold, as no one will take up the bidding. On the other hand, a majority of those that are sold go for the minimum, which may be very low.

Part-time auctioneers. They do not have the clientele or experience to do a good job on your collection. It takes many years of experience to catalog correctly, build a reputation, and get lots of active bidding from both dealers and collectors.

Choice of a dealer to buy outright or sell at auction. Every dealer will tell you how great and honest he is. Some will knock their competitors (beware of these!). The best test if you don't know any is to check his references, his bank, and his Dun & Bradstreet ratings. Also, get the names of half a dozen other collectors who have actually done business with him and find out whether they were satisfied.

It's not very nice to consign a collection to a dealer for outright sale or auction and have to wait and wait to get paid. If it's a cash sale, don't take it in installments; that can go on for years, the cream may then be gone, and you may have to take back what's left that the dealer couldn't sell.

Check the promptness with which your auctioneer will pay. We know a collector who sold an $80,000 collection at auction and had to travel 700 miles each month to get $10,000 each trip, when he should have been paid outright in thirty days.

20. COIN VALUES ARE DETERMINED BY DEMAND AND CONDITION

New collectors take up the hobby of coin collecting every day. Older coins disappear from circulation very quickly and the supply coming into the market from the break-up of collections cannot keep pace with the demand that comes from ever greater numbers of collectors of American coins. Thus, the demand for these coins grows while the supply diminishes. The result has been a steadily rising level in the value of American coins.

Besides rarity, however, there is another factor that affects a coin's value, namely, its state of preservation or condition. Collectors will often pay many times as much for a coin in superior condition than for a specimen that is just average.

The prices listed in this book are, for the most part, for "fine" coins. A "fine" coin is one that shows a reasonable amount of wear but is still a desirable coin. The basic outline is still clear but much of the fine detail is worn away. All lettering should be legible. The next grade below this is "very good," a much worn but not altogether unattractive coin. A coin in this condition should be free of serious gouges or other mutilations but it may be somewhat scratched from use. A coin that is rated only "good" is really a minimum condition coin. The date and mint mark would be legible and the major portions of the design distinguishable. "Fair" indicates a badly worn coin that is usually not acceptable to a collector. "Fair" coins are generally used as "space fillers," only until such time as a better coin can be acquired.

The grade above "fine" is "very fine," a coin on which the design is still quite clear and which over all shows the very slightest amount of wear. An "extremely fine" coin shows the slightest signs of wear or rubbing only on the very highest points of the design. "Uncirculated" indicates a coin absolutely without wear. Above "uncirculated" is "proof," a coin which is a special coin with a mirror-like surface especially minted for collectors. The "proof" coin must be absolutely perfect.

There is no iron-bound rule as to values but the following pages should give you an *approximate* idea of what your coins are worth. The values shown are the prices the dealers charge when they sell coins. If a "fine" coin as listed in this book is listed at $10, you can expect dealers to pay you between 50 and 70 percent of the price shown. This will, of course, depend upon how badly the dealer needs the coin or coins. Dealers usually carry a large stock of coins and cannot be expected to pay high prices for those items that they have a lot of. On the other hand, if he needs your coin badly, he often will pay record prices.

Part Two:
THE COINS LISTED

ABBREVIATIONS USED IN THE COIN VALUE LISTS

Unc.—Uncirculated
Ex. Fine—Extremely Fine
V. Fine—Very Fine
V. Good—Very Good

More detailed information about minor varieties can be found in the following books:

A Guide Book of U.S. Coins, Whitman Publishing Co. General information.
Miller-Ryder, *The State Coinages of New England.* Colonial Coins.
Dr. Edward Maris, *New Jersey Cents.* Colonial Coins.
Sydney P. Noe, *The New England and Willow Tree Coinages of Massachusetts.* Colonial Coins.
S. S. Crosby, *Cents and Half Cents of 1793.*
Gilbert Elder, *U.S. Half Cents.*
Wm. H. Sheldon, *Penny Whimsey.* Large cents.
D. W. Valentine, *U.S. Half Dimes.*
J. W. Haseltine, *Type table of U.S. Dollars, Halves and Quarters.*
M. H. Bolender, *Silver Dollars 1794–1804.*

21.

COLONIAL COINS BEFORE THE DECLARATION OF INDEPENDENCE: 1652–1776

MASSACHUSETTS

NEW ENGLAND PIECES

Shilling

	Good	*Fine*	*Ex. Fine*
NE Shilling	2,500.00	6,500.00	–
NE Sixpence (Very rare)	–	–	–
NE Threepence (2 known, very rare)	–	–	–

WILLOW TREE PIECES

Willow Tree Shilling	1,000.00	3,000.00	–
Willow Tree Sixpence	3,000.00	–	–
Willow Tree Threepence (3 known, very rare)	–	–	–

OAK TREE PIECES

Oak Tree Shilling	200.00	325.00	–
Oak Tree Sixpence	200.00	350.00	–
Oak Tree Threepence	200.00	350.00	–
Oak Tree Twopence (1662)	200.00	300.00	–

PINE TREE PIECES

Pine Tree Shilling, Large Planchet	200.00	300.00	–
Pine Tree Shilling, Small Planchet	200.00	275.00	–
Pine Tree Sixpence	225.00	275.00	–
Pine Tree Threepence	225.00	275.00	–

MARYLAND (1658)

LORD BALTIMORE COINAGE

Shilling	750.00	1,500.00	–
Sixpence	500.00	900.00	–
Fourpence	600.00	1,000.00	–

NEW JERSEY

MARK NEWBY COINAGE

St. Patrick Halfpence	100.00	200.00	–
St. Patrick Farthing with Brass Plug on Obverse	75.00	150.00	–
St. Patrick Farthing without Brass Plug	75.00	150.00	–
St. Patrick Farthing, Silver	450.00	750.00	–

FLORIDA TOKEN

	Good	Fine	Unc.
(1688) Florida, James II Plantation Token, 1/24 part real – Pewter	30.00	50.00	150.00

CAROLINA ELEPHANT TOKENS

	Good	Fine	–
1694 PROPRIETORS (3 known)	–	–	–
1694 PROPRIETORS	250.00	500.00	–
(1694) Halfpenny GOD PRESERVE LONDON (Thick Planchet)	50.00	100.00	–
(1694) Halfpenny GOD PRESERVE LONDON (Thin Planchet)	60.00	110.00	–
(1694) Halfpenny GOD PRESERVE LONDON (Diagonals in center of shield)	100.00	200.00	–
(1694) Halfpenny, similar. Variety with sword in second quarter of shield instead of first (rare)	–	–	–
(1694) Halfpenny LONDON	100.00	200.00	–

NEW ENGLAND

1694 NEW ENGLAND (Very rare)	–	–	–

FRENCH COLONIES

1721 Mint Mark B, Sou	22.50	50.00	–
1721 Mint Mark H, Sou	20.00	30.00	–
1722 Sou	12.50	25.00	–
1767 Sou	20.00	40.00	–
1767 Sou Counterstamp "R.F."	10.00	20.00	–

WILLIAM WOOD'S COINAGE

ROSA AMERICANA

	Good	Fine	Ex.Fine
Twopence (no date)	35.00	100.00	150.00
1722 Twopence, Period after REX	35.00	100.00	150.00
1722 Twopence, No Period after REX	35.00	100.00	150.00
1722 Penny UTILE DULCI	30.00	60.00	115.00
1722 Penny VTILE DVLCI	20.00	50.00	100.00
1722 Halfpenny D.G. REX ROSA AMERI. UTILE DULCI	30.00	70.00	140.00
1722 Halfpenny DEI GRATIA REX UTILE DULCI	30.00	60.00	100.00
1722 Halfpenny VTILE DVLCI	–	–	–
1723 Twopence	30.00	75.00	125.00
1723 Penny	30.00	60.00	110.00
1723 Halfpenny	30.00	60.00	110.00
1723 Halfpenny Uncrowned Rose	50.00	100.00	200.00
1724 Penny	–	–	–
1724 Penny (Undated) ROSA:SINE: SPINA. (3 known)	–	–	–

HIBERNIA

1722 Halfpenny, First Type, Harp at Left	20.00	40.00	80.00
1722 Halfpenny, Second Type, Harp at Right	20.00	55.00	105.00

	Good	Fine	Ex.Fine
1723 Halfpenny	12.50	30.00	60.00
1723 over 22 Halfpenny	30.00	65.00	125.00
1723 Farthing	12.50	30.00	60.00
1724 Halfpenny	12.50	35.00	70.00
1724 Farthing	20.00	40.00	85.00

HIGLEY COPPERS

	V. Fair	Good	–
1737 THE•VALVE•OF•THREE•PENCE.–3 Hammers CONNECTICVT	4,000.00	5,000.00	–
1737 THE•VALVE•OF•THREE•PENCE.–3 Hammers–I•AM•GOOD•COPPER	4,000.00	5,000.00	–
1737 VALUE•ME•AS•YOU•PLEASE–3 Hammers–I•AM•GOOD•COPPER	4,000.00	5,000.00	–
1737 VALVE•ME•AS•YOU•PLEASE–3 Hammers–I•AM•GOOD•COPPER	4,000.00	5,000.00	–
(1737) VALUE•ME•AS•YOU•PLEASE–Broad Axe–J•CUT•MY•WAY• THROUGH	4,000.00	5,000.00	–
(1737) Similar, Wheel Design (Unique)	–	–	–
1739 VALUE•ME•AS•YOU•PLEASE–Broad Axe–J•CUT•MY•WAY• THROUGH	4,000.00	5,000.00	–

VOCE POPULI

	Good	Fine	–
1700 Halfpenny	–	–	–
1760 Halfpenny	17.00	35.00	–
1760 Halfpenny VOOE POPULI	35.00	70.00	–
1760 Farthing Large Letters	65.00	125.00	–
1760 Farthing Small Letters	–	–	–

PITT TOKEN

	Good	Fine	Ex. Fine
1766 Halfpenny	30.00	70.00	150.00
1766 Farthing	–	–	–

VIRGINIA

	Good	Fine	Unc.
1733 Halfpenny, Period after GEORGIUS	10.00	20.00	50.00
1773 Halfpenny, No period after GEORGIUS	20.00	45.00	90.00

22.

STATE COINAGE

CONNECTICUT CENTS

	Good	Fine	–
1785 Bust Right	10.00	20.00	–
1785 Bust Left	25.00	75.00	–
1786 Bust Right	25.00	60.00	–
1786 Bust Left	15.00	30.00	–
1786 Draped Bust	25.00	50.00	–
1787 Mailed Bust Right	10.00	20.00	–
1787 Mailed Bust Left	10.00	20.00	–
1787 Draped Bust Left	7.50	15.00	–
1788 Mailed Bust Right	15.00	30.00	–
1788 Mailed Bust Left	15.00	30.00	–
1788 Draped Bust Left	15.00	30.00	–

(Note: There are many minor varieties of Connecticut Cents.)

MASSACHUSETTS

	Good	Fine	Ex. Fine
1787 Cent, Arrows in Right Talon (Ex.rare)	–	–	–
1787 Cent, Arrows in Left Talon	10.00	25.00	75.00
1787 Cent, Horn (Die Break) from Eagle's Head	15.00	25.00	75.00
1787 Half Cent	15.00	30.00	85.00
1788 Cent	12.50	25.00	75.00
1788 Half Cent	17.50	35.00	90.00

NEW HAMPSHIRE

1776 New Hampshire Halfpenny (Very rare)	–	–	–

NEW JERSEY CENTS

	Good	Fine	–
1786 IMMUNIS COLUMBIA (Very rare)	–	–	–
1786 Date under Plow Handle (Very rare)	–	–	–
1786 No Coulter	55.00	110.00	–
1786 Narrow or Wide Shield	10.00	25.00	–
1787 Small or Large Planchet	10.00	25.00	–
1787 Outlined Shield	10.00	25.00	–
1787 Plurибs instead of Pluribus	20.00	40.00	–
1788 Horse head Right	10.00	20.00	–
1788 Horse head Left	35.00	70.00	–

(Note: There are many minor varieties of New Jersey Cents.)

NEW YORK CENTS

	Good	Fine	V. Fine
1786 NON VI VIRTUTE VICI	400.00	700.00	1,200.00
1787 Excelsior Cent, Eagle Right	225.00	450.00	900.00
1787 Excelsior Cent, Eagle Left	200.00	400.00	800.00
1787 Excelsior Cent, Large Eagle (Very rare)	—	—	—
1787 Excelsior, Indian	375.00	750.00	1,500.00
1787 Excelsior George Clinton	400.00	800.00	1,750.00
1787 Indian, Eagle on Globe	500.00	1,000.00	2,000.00
1787 IMMUNIS COLUMBIA	80.00	100.00	200.00
1787 NOVA-EBORAC, Figure Left	30.00	60.00	100.00
1787 NOVA-EBORAC, Figure Right	30.00	60.00	100.00
1787 NOVA-EBORAC, Small Head	150.00	300.00	450.00
1787 NOVA-EBORAC, Large Head	60.00	120.00	250.00

VERMONT CENTS

	Good	Fine	—
1785 IMMUNE COLUMBIA	300.00	600.00	—
1785 Mountain Scene, VERMONTS	50.00	100.00	—
1785 Mountain Scene, VERMONTIS	75.00	150.00	—
1786 Mountain Scene, VERMONTENSIUM	50.00	100.00	—
1786 Baby Head	50.00	110.00	—
1786 Bust Left	30.00	100.00	—
1787 Bust Left	400.00	800.00	—
1787 Bust Right	20.00	50.00	—
1787 BRITANNIA on Reverse	15.00	50.00	—
1788	20.00	50.00	—
1788 GEORGIUS III REX	30.00	75.00	—

EXPERIMENTAL COINS

CONTINENTAL DOLLAR

	Good	Fine	Ex. Fine
1776 CURENCY, Pewter	400.00	600.00	900.00
1776 CURENCY, Brass (Very rare)	—	—	—
1776 CURENCY, Silver (Very rare)	—	—	—
1776 CURRENCY, Pewter	400.00	600.00	900.00
1776 CURRENCY, Pewter, E.G. Fecit	600.00	900.00	1,200.00

	Good	Fine	Ex. Fine
1776 CURRENCY, Silver, E.G. Fecit (Very rare)....	–	–	–
1776 CURRENCEY, Pewter (Very rare)................	–	–	–

NOVA CONSTELLATIO (SILVER)

	Good	Fine	Ex. Fine
1783 MARK (1000), Silver (Unique).....................	–	–	–
1783 QUINT (500), Silver–Type 1 (Unique)..........	–	–	–
1783 QUINT (500), Silver–Type 2 (Unique)..........	–	–	–
1783 Bit (100), Silver (2 known)............................	–	–	–

NOVA CONSTELLATIO CENTS

	Good	Fine	Ex. Fine
1783 CONSTELLATIO, Small U.S.	10.00	20.00	50.00
1783 CONSTELLATIO, Large U.S.	10.00	30.00	60.00
1783 CONSTELATIO, Blunt Rays	10.00	20.00	60.00
1785 CONSTELATIO, Blunt Rays	20.00	40.00	90.00
1785 CONSTELLATIO, Pointed Rays..................	10.00	25.00	50.00
1786 CONSTELLATIO (Very rare).......................	–	–	–

IMMUNE COLUMBIA CENTS

	Good	*Fine*	*V. Fine*
1785 CONSTELLATIO.......................................	250.00	500.00	1,000.00
1785 CONSTELATIO (Very rare) Known in Copper and Gold	–	–	–
1785 George III Obverse	250.00	500.00	Unknown

CONFEDERATIO CENTS

1785 Stars in Large or Small Circle (All very rare) ...	–	–	–

THE FUGIO CENTS

	Good	*Fine*	*Ex. Fine*
1787 Club Rays...	40.00	75.00	150.00

POINTED RAYS

1787 UNITED above STATES below (Very rare) ...	–	–	–
1787 UNITED STATES at sides of circle	20.00	40.00	100.00

1787 STATES UNITED at sides of circle	20.00	40.00	90.00

(Note: There are several minor varieties of the Fugio Cents.)

23.

FIRST MINT ISSUES

	Good	Fine	Unc.
1792 DISME known in Silver and Copper (Very rare)	–	–	–

	Good	Fine	Ex. Fine
1792 HALF DISME, Silver	600.00	1,200.00	2,000.00
1792 HALF DISME, Copper (Very rare)	–	–	–
1792 Silver Center Cent (Very rare)	–	–	–
1792 BIRCH CENT (Very rare)	–	–	–

MISCELLANEOUS TOKENS

RHODE ISLAND SHIP TOKEN

1778 Wreath below Ship	–	85.00	175.00
1778 No wreath	–	80.00	170.00

NORTH AMERICAN TOKEN

	Good	Fine	–
1781	10.00	20.00	–

GEORGIUS TRIUMPHO TOKEN

1783 GEORGIUS TRIUMPHO	25.00	50.00	–

J. CHALMERS

ANNAPOLIS, MARYLAND

1783 Shilling–Birds, Long or Short Worm	175.00	350.00	–
1783 Shilling–Rings (Ex. rare)	–	–	–
1783 Sixpence, Small Date	300.00	600.00	–
1783 Sixpence, Large Date	250.00	500.00	–
1783 Threepence	200.00	400.00	–

THE BAR CENT

	Good	Fine	Unc.
Undated (1785) Bar Cent	150.00	225.00	500.00

	Good	Fine	Unc.
AUCTORI PLEBIS TOKEN			
1787	25.00	60.00	–
BRASHER'S DOUBLOONS			
1787 "E.B." on Breast or Wing (All very rare)	–	–	–

THE MOTT TOKEN

	Good	Fine	Ex. Fine
1789 Mott Token, Thick Planchet	20.00	35.00	90.00
1789 Mott Token, Thin Planchet	30.00	50.00	115.00
STANDISH BARRY, BALTIMORE, MARYLAND			
1790 Threepence (Very rare)	–	–	–

KENTUCKY TOKEN

	V.Good	V. Fine	Unc.
Cent (1792) Plain Edge	16.00	30.00	90.00
Cent, Engrailed Edge	50.00	100.00	300.00
Cent, Lettered Edge	20.00	40.00	125.00

FRANKLIN PRESS CENT

	Good	Fine	Unc.
1794	20.00	50.00	90.00
TALBOT ALLUM & LEE CENTS			
1794 With NEW YORK	10.00	30.00	90.00
1794 Without NEW YORK	70.00	250.00	500.00
1795	10.00	20.00	60.00
MYDDELTON TOKENS			
1796 Copper. Proof only	–	–	850.00
1796 Silver. Proof only	–	–	850.00

WASHINGTON CENTS

	Good	Fine	Ex. Fine
1783 WASHINGTON & INDEPENDENCE Small Military bust	12.00	20.00	50.00
1783 Same, Engrailed Edge	12.50	25.00	75.00
1783 Large Military bust	10.00	20.00	50.00
1783 Draped bust	10.00	17.50	30.00
1783 Draped bust with button	25.00	40.00	80.00
1783 Restrike in Copper. Proof only. Plain Edge	–	–	125.00
1783 Restrike in Copper. Proof only. Engrailed Edge	–	–	50.00
1783 Restrike in Silver. Proof only. Engrailed Edge	–	–	150.00
1783 UNITY STATES	10.00	20.00	50.00
(1783) Double Head Cent	15.00	35.00	75.00
1784 Ugly Head (Very rare)	–	–	–

	Good	Fine	Unc.
1791 Small Eagle	50.00	100.00	200.00
1791 Large Eagle	35.00	75.00	175.00
1792 WASHINGTON PRESIDENT	–	1,100.00	–
(1792) WASHINGTON BORN VIRGINIA	–	1,100.00	–
		1,000.00	

	Good	Fine	Unc.
1792 Roman Head (Rare). Proof only–750.00			
1795 Grate Cent, Lettered edge	100.00	200.00	400.00
1795 Grate Cent, Reeded edge	20.00	40.00	100.00

WASHINGTON PENNIES AND HALFPENNIES

	Good	Fine	Unc.
(1795) Penny, Lettered edge "LIBERTY & SECURITY"	30.00	50.00	150.00
1791 LIVERPOOL HALFPENNY	150.00	300.00	400.00

	Good	Fine	Ex. Fine
1793 Ship Halfpenny	20.00	35.00	80.00
1795 Halfpenny, Plain edge	30.00	50.00	115.00
1795 Halfpenny, Lettered edge	20.00	30.00	60.00
1795 Halfpenny, Edge "AN ASYLUM FOR THE OPPRESSED OF ALL NATIONS"	50.00	100.00	200.00
1795 NORTH WALES Halfpenny	35.00	90.00	–
SUCCESS Token Large, Plain & Reeded edge	30.00	75.00	–
SUCCESS Token Small, Plain & Reeded edge	30.00	75.00	–

WASHINGTON HALF DOLLARS

	Good	Fine	Unc.
1792 Silver Half Dollar (Very rare)	–	10,000.00	–
1792 Silver, Ornamental edge (Very rare)	–	15,000.00	–
1792 Copper	–	–	4,000.00
1792 Copper, Ornamental edge	–	–	5,000.00

24.
HALF-CENT PIECES—
1793–1857

LIBERTY CAP TYPE

1793

1794–1797

	Good	Fine	V. Fine
1793	250.00	1,000.00	1,500.00
1794	75.00	200.00	300.00
1795 Lettered Edge, Pole to Cap	75.00	175.00	250.00
1795 Plain Edge, No Pole to Cap	60.00	175.00	250.00
1796 Plain Edge, Pole	1,000.00	2,500.00	3,500.00
1796 Plain Edge, No Pole	1,000.00	2,500.00	3,750.00
1797 Plain Edge	75.00	150.00	250.00
1797 Lettered Edge	200.00	500.00	850.00

DRAPED BUST TYPE

1800	10.00	25.00	35.00
1802 (Over 1800)	75.00	185.00	350.00
1803	10.00	20.00	30.00
1804 Stemless Wreath	6.00	12.00	20.00
1804 Stems to Wreath	6.00	12.00	20.00
1805 Small 5, Stemless Wreath	10.00	20.00	30.00
1805 Stems to Wreath	7.00	15.00	30.00
1806 Stemless	7.00	12.00	25.00

	Good	Fine	V. Fine
1806 Stems	7.00	12.00	25.00
1807	7.00	12.00	25.00
1808 over 7	50.00	80.00	160.00
1808	7.00	15.00	30.00

TURBAN HEAD TYPE

	Good	Fine	V. Fine
1809 over 6	10.00	20.00	30.00
1809	10.00	15.00	20.00
1810	15.00	30.00	50.00
1811	40.00	80.00	150.00

	Good	Fine	V. Fine	Unc.
1825	7.00	12.00	20.00	60.00
1826	7.00	12.00	20.00	60.00
1828 13 Stars	6.00	10.00	20.00	60.00
1828 12 Stars	7.00	20.00	50.00	150.00
1829	6.00	12.00	25.00	60.00

	V.Good	Fine	V. Fine	Unc.	Proof
1831	–	–	–	–	800.00
1832	7.50	10.00	17.50	50.00	600.00
1833	6.00	10.00	17.00	50.00	400.00
1834	6.00	10.00	17.00	50.00	400.00
1835	6.00	10.00	17.00	50.00	400.00
1836 Original	–	–	–	–	450.00

BRAIDED HAIR TYPE

	Fine	V. Fine	Unc.	Proof
1849 Large Date	18.00	27.50	100.00	–
1850	15.00	22.00	60.00	–
1851	10.00	20.00	60.00	–
1852 Proof only	–	–	–	500.00
1853	10.00	20.00	60.00	–
1854	11.00	20.00	60.00	700.00

	Fine	*V. Fine*	*Unc.*	*Proof*
1855	11.00	20.00	60.00	375.00
1856	12.00	20.00	60.00	400.00
1857	15.00	30.00	85.00	400.00

25.
ONE-CENT PIECES–
1793–1857

CHAIN TYPE

	Good	Fine	V. Fine	Unc.
1793 Chain type, AMERI	500.00	1,000.00	1,600.00	–
1793 Chain type, AMERICA	450.00	900.00	1,300.00	–

WREATH TYPE

1793 Wreath Type, Vine and Bars on Edge..	200.00	450.00	900.00	4,000.00
1793 Wreath type, Lettered Edge	250.00	500.00	1,000.00	–

LIBERTY CAP TYPE

	Good	Fine	V. Fine	Unc.
1793 Liberty Cap type	750.00	1,500.00	2,500.00	–
1794	35.00	100.00	175.00	2,100.00
1795 Lettered Edge..............................	40.00	125.00	200.00	2,300.00
1795 Plain Edge	30.00	70.00	120.00	850.00
1796 Liberty Cap type	50.00	100.00	200.00	–

DRAPED BUST TYPE

	Good	Fine	V. Fine	Unc.
1796 Draped bust type	35.00	90.00	180.00	1,250.00
1797 Stems on Wreath	20.00	40.00	75.00	525.00
1797 Stemless Wreath	50.00	125.00	225.00	1,300.00
1798 over 97	25.00	80.00	140.00	4,200.00
1798	7.50	17.50	30.00	500.00
1799 over 98	325.00	1,200.00	2,100.00	–
1799	300.00	1,000.00	2,000.00	–
1800 over 1798	12.50	30.00	60.00	–
1800 over 179......................................	10.00	30.00	60.00	–
1800	10.00	25.00	50.00	1,800.00
1801	10.00	25.00	50.00	500.00
1801 3 errors– 1/000, one stem and IINITED	30.00	100.00	190.00	–
1801 Fraction 1/000	17.00	40.00	75.00	2,200.00
1801 Fraction 1/100 over 1/000	20.00	50.00	100.00	–
1802	8.00	17.00	40.00	1,600.00
1802 Stemless Wreath	11.00	25.00	40.00	650.00
1802 Fraction 1/000	12.00	27.00	60.00	750.00
1803	10.00	20.00	45.00	1,150.00
1803 Stemless Wreath	15.00	40.00	75.00	2,800.00
1803 1/100 over 1/000	20.00	50.00	100.00	2,000.00

	Good	Fine	V. Fine	Unc.
1804	200.00	450.00	800.00	–
1805	10.00	25.00	40.00	750.00
1806	20.00	60.00	100.00	2,500.00
1807 over 6	10.00	25.00	50.00	1,350.00
1807	10.00	20.00	40.00	3,200.00

TURBAN HEAD TYPE

1808 13 Stars	15.00	45.00	85.00	1,850.00
1808 12 Stars	16.00	45.00	90.00	1,100.00
1809	75.00	200.00	300.00	–
1810 over 9	12.50	30.00	50.00	–
1810	10.00	25.00	60.00	–
1811 over 10	50.00	125.00	250.00	–
1811	50.00	120.00	240.00	2,200.00
1812	10.00	25.00	50.00	950.00
1813	25.00	60.00	100.00	625.00
1814	10.00	25.00	50.00	600.00

CORONET TYPE

1816	4.00	10.00	20.00	100.00
1817	4.00	10.00	17.50	90.00
1817 15 Stars	7.50	20.00	30.00	150.00
1818	4.00	10.00	17.50	85.00
1819 over 18	5.00	12.00	20.00	175.00
1819 Small Date	3.50	10.00	15.00	90.00
1820 over 19	3.50	10.00	15.00	125.00
1820	3.00	9.00	15.00	100.00
1821	10.00	30.00	60.00	2,000.00
1822	4.00	10.00	20.00	150.00
1823 over 22	20.00	50.00	100.00	1,300.00

	Good	Fine	V. Fine	Unc.
1823	25.00	65.00	125.00	2,100.00
1824 over 22	10.00	27.50	50.00	400.00
1824	5.00	15.00	25.00	225.00
1825	5.00	10.00	25.00	175.00
1826 over 25	9.50	30.00	60.00	225.00
1826	4.00	10.00	20.00	140.00
1827	3.50	10.00	15.00	125.00
1828	3.50	10.00	15.00	135.00
1829	3.50	10.00	15.00	125.00
1830	3.50	7.50	11.50	140.00
1831	3.50	7.50	12.00	120.00
1832	3.50	7.50	12.00	100.00
1833	3.50	7.50	12.00	100.00
1834	5.00	15.00	20.00	170.00
1835 Type of '34	5.00	15.00	25.00	100.00
1835 Type of '36	4.00	10.00	15.00	100.00
1836	3.50	10.00	15.00	115.00
1837 Plain Hair Cord	4.00	15.00	22.00	135.00
1837 Beaded Hair Cord	3.50	8.50	11.00	90.00
1838	3.50	7.00	11.00	85.00
1839 over 36 Line under CENT, No dot	100.00	250.00	400.00	1,000.00
1839 Type of '38, Line under cent	7.00	15.00	25.00	150.00
1839 Silly Head, Line under CENT; No center dot	10.00	20.00	30.00	200.00
1839 Booby Head, no line under CENT	6.00	15.00	25.00	150.00
1839 Type of '40, no line under CENT	7.00	20.00	25.00	160.00

BRAIDED HAIR TYPE

	Good	Fine	V. Fine	Unc.
1840	4.00	9.00	14.00	100.00
1841	4.00	9.00	14.00	110.00
1842	4.00	9.00	14.00	105.00
1843 Obverse and Reverse of 1842	4.00	9.00	14.00	100.00
1843 Obverse of 1842, Reverse of '44	15.00	50.00	75.00	450.00
1843 Obverse and Reverse of 1844	6.00	12.00	20.00	150.00
1844	3.00	6.00	10.00	90.00
1844/81	6.00	10.00	30.00	150.00
1845	3.00	5.00	8.00	75.00
1846	3.00	5.00	8.00	90.00
1847	3.00	5.00	8.00	70.00
1848	3.00	5.00	8.00	65.00
1849	3.00	5.00	8.00	65.00
1850	3.00	5.00	8.00	65.00
1851	3.00	5.00	8.00	65.00

	Good	*Fine*	*V. Fine*	*Unc.*
1851/81	6.50	16.00	35.00	200.00
1852	3.00	5.00	8.00	60.00
1853	3.00	5.00	8.00	60.00
1854	3.00	5.00	8.00	60.00
1855	3.00	5.00	8.00	70.00
1856	3.00	5.00	8.00	70.00
1857	20.00	30.00	40.00	140.00

FLYING EAGLE CENTS—1856–1858

COPPER-NICKEL ("WHITE" CENTS)

	Good	*Fine*	*V. Fine*	*Unc.*	*Proof*
1856	500.00	700.00	900.00	1,700.00	2,000.00
1857	4.00	8.00	13.00	75.00	900.00
1858 Large Letters	4.00	9.00	15.00	110.00	1,000.00
1858 Small Letters	4.00	9.00	15.00	110.00	1,000.00

INDIAN HEAD CENTS—1859–1864

COPPER-NICKEL OR "WHITE"

1859

1860–1864

1859	2.50	7.00	10.00	60.00	400.00
1860	2.00	6.00	8.00	37.50	300.00
1861	6.00	11.50	16.00	65.00	350.00
1862	1.75	3.50	5.00	15.00	200.00
1863	1.50	3.00	5.00	15.00	200.00
1864	3.75	9.00	12.50	35.00	360.00

1864–1909 BRONZE

	Good	Fine	V. Fine	Unc.	Proof
1864 No L Bronze	1.00	5.00	10.00	40.00	500.00
1864 L on ribbon	12.00	45.00	60.00	200.00	—
1865	1.50	6.00	6.50	25.00	200.00
1866	5.00	15.00	30.00	95.00	250.00
1867	6.50	12.50	27.50	100.00	300.00
1868	6.50	20.00	37.50	125.00	250.00
1869 over 8	35.00	75.00	95.00	475.00	—
1869	11.00	45.00	62.50	250.00	400.00
1870	11.00	35.00	45.00	125.00	300.00
1871	15.00	40.00	60.00	150.00	350.00
1872	17.00	50.00	75.00	250.00	450.00
1873	4.00	10.00	20.00	75.00	200.00
1874	3.00	10.00	20.00	75.00	150.00
1875	3.00	10.00	20.00	75.00	150.00
1876	5.00	15.00	27.00	85.00	140.00
1877	80.00	175.00	230.00	750.00	1,000.00
1878	6.00	17.00	27.50	75.00	125.00
1879	1.50	5.00	7.00	25.00	60.00
1880	.75	3.00	5.00	20.00	50.00
1881	.75	3.00	5.00	20.00	50.00
1882	.75	3.00	5.00	20.00	50.00
1883	.75	3.00	4.50	15.00	50.00
1884	1.50	4.00	7.50	25.00	50.00
1885	3.00	9.00	14.00	40.00	50.00
1886	1.75	5.00	9.00	27.50	60.00
1887	.40	1.75	3.00	15.00	50.00
1888	.40	1.75	4.00	20.00	40.00
1889	.40	1.75	3.00	15.00	40.00
1890	.40	1.75	3.00	15.00	40.00
1891	.40	1.75	3.00	15.00	40.00
1892	.40	1.75	3.00	16.00	40.00
1893	.40	1.75	3.00	15.00	40.00
1894	1.00	6.00	10.00	20.00	50.00
1895	.35	1.50	3.00	15.00	40.00
1896	.35	1.50	3.00	20.00	50.00
1897	.35	1.50	3.00	15.00	45.00
1898	.35	1.50	3.00	15.00	45.00
1899	.30	.75	1.50	15.00	35.00
1900	.30	.75	1.50	7.50	25.00
1901	.30	.75	1.50	6.50	25.00
1902	.30	.75	1.50	6.50	25.00
1903	.30	.75	1.50	6.50	25.00
1904	.30	.75	1.50	6.50	25.00
1905	.30	.75	1.50	6.50	25.00

	Good	Fine	V. Fine	Unc.	Proof
1906	.30	.75	1.50	6.50	25.00
1907	.30	.75	1.50	6.50	27.50
1908	.30	.75	1.50	7.50	26.00
1908S	15.00	20.00	30.00	100.00	–
1909	.50	1.50	2.50	8.00	27.50
1909S	65.00	85.00	110.00	250.00	–

LINCOLN HEAD CENTS—1909–Date

1909–1958 1959–1964

1909 V D B	.50	.75	1.00	5.00	200.00
1909S, V D B	60.00	90.00	110.00	175.00	–
1909	.15	.40	.65	5.00	65.00
1909S	7.50	15.00	25.00	50.00	–
1910	.10	.15	.70	6.50	60.00
1910S	2.50	4.00	6.00	30.00	–
1911	.10	.15	.75	8.00	70.00
1911D	1.00	1.50	5.00	24.00	–
1911S	6.00	10.00	13.00	40.00	–
1912	.10	.75	1.00	10.00	70.00
1912D	1.25	4.25	7.00	37.50	–
1912S	3.00	6.00	9.00	40.00	–
1913	.10	.25	.75	10.00	60.00
1913D	.50	1.50	4.00	35.00	–
1913S	2.00	4.00	6.00	40.00	–
1914	.15	.75	1.75	20.00	125.00
1914D	30.00	50.00	80.00	450.00	–
1914S	3.00	5.00	9.00	75.00	–
1915	.40	1.50	6.00	20.00	200.00
1915D	.40	.80	2.50	17.50	–
1915S	2.00	3.00	7.00	40.00	–
1916	.10	.15	1.00	6.00	210.00
1916D	.20	.75	1.75	17.00	–
1916S	.45	.75	1.80	25.00	–
1917	.10	.15	1.00	9.00	–
1917D	.25	.75	1.75	20.00	–
1917S	.25	.75	1.75	20.00	–
1918	.10	.15	.65	8.00	–
1918D	.25	1.00	1.50	25.00	–
1918S	.25	1.00	1.50	25.00	–
1919	.10	.15	.65	7.00	–
1919D	.15	.40	1.00	16.50	–
1919S	.15	.40	1.00	16.50	–
1920	.10	.15	.75	6.00	–
1920D	.15	.45	1.25	30.00	–
1920S	.15	.45	1.40	30.00	–
1921	.15	.50	1.00	20.00	–

	Good	*Fine*	*V. Fine*	*Unc.*	*Proof*
1921S	.50	1.60	4.00	145.00	–
1922D	2.50	4.00	7.50	40.00	–
1922 No "D"	35.00	50.00	90.00	500.00	–

	Good	*Fine*	*V. Fine*	*Unc.*
1923	.10	.15	.85	6.50
1923S	.90	2.00	5.00	210.00
1924	.10	.20	1.00	12.50
1924D	7.50	12.00	20.00	160.00
1924S	.50	1.25	3.00	75.00
1925	.10	.15	.50	5.00
1925D	.20	.30	1.00	22.50
1925S	.20	.30	1.00	25.00
1926	.10	.15	.50	3.35
1926D	.15	.25	.75	20.00
1926S	1.25	4.00	6.00	95.00
1927	.10	.15	.50	4.00
1927D	.15	.20	.75	18.50
1927S	.30	.40	1.00	35.00
1928	.10	.15	.50	3.00
1928D	.10	.35	.60	14.00
1928S	.25	.60	1.00	24.00
1929	.10	.20	.40	3.50
1929D	.10	.20	.40	6.80
1929S	.10	.20	.40	4.00
1930	.10	.20	.40	3.00
1930D	.10	.25	.45	5.00
1930S	.10	.25	.45	5.50
1931	.25	.40	.80	10.00
1931D	2.00	3.50	4.50	30.00
1931S	7.50	15.00	25.00	40.00
1932	.40	1.15	1.50	8.00
1932D	.40	1.10	1.50	8.00
1933	.40	.50	1.00	12.00
1933D	1.25	2.00	3.00	15.00
1934	–	–	–	2.50
1934D	–	–	–	8.50
1935	–	–	–	1.00
1935D	–	–	–	2.50
1935S	–	–	–	3.50
1936	–	–	–	.75
1936D	–	–	–	2.00
1936S	–	–	–	2.50
1937	–	–	–	.75
1937D	–	–	–	1.25
1937S	–	–	–	1.60
1938	–	–	–	1.50
1938D	–	–	–	2.25
1938S	–	–	–	3.00
1939	–	–	–	.75
1939D	–	–	.65	3.00
1939S	–	–	–	1.25
1940	–	–	–	.60
1940D	–	–	–	1.00
1940S	–	–	–	.80

	Unc.
1941	.60
1941D	1.00
1941S	1.00
1942	.40
1942D	.40
1942S	3.00
1943 Steel	.50
1943D Steel	.70
1943S Steel	1.25
1944 Copper	.40
1944D	.30
1944S	.40
1945	.35
1945D	.40
1945S	.50
1946	.25
1946D	.30
1946S	.40
1947	.50
1947D	.60
1947S	.65
1948	.40
1948D	.40
1948S	.50
1949	.65
1949D	.65
1949S	1.50
1950	.40
1950D	.40
1950S	.75
1951	.50
1951D	.30
1951S	.90
1952	.55
1952D	.35
1952S	.60
1953	.35
1953D	.35
1953S	.50
1954	.60
1954D	.30
1954S	.40
1955	.25

	Good	*Fine*	*Unc.*
1955 Doubled Die Obverse	175.00	225.00	400.00
1955D	—	—	.20
1955S	—	—	.75
1956	—	—	.15
1956D	—	—	.10
1957	—	—	.10
1957D	—	—	.10
1958	—	—	.15
1958D	—	—	.10

MEMORIAL REVERSE TYPE

1959	—	—	.10

	Good	Fine	Unc.
1959D	–	–	.10
1960 Large Date	–	–	.10
1960 Small Date	–	–	5.00
1960D Large Date	–	–	.10
1960D Small Date	–	–	.50
1961	–	–	.05
1961D	–	–	.05
1962	–	–	.05
1962D	–	–	.05
1963	–	–	.05
1963D	–	–	.05
1964	–	–	.05
1964D	–	–	.05
1965	–	–	.05
1966	–	–	.05
1967	–	–	.05
1968	–	–	.05
1968D	–	–	.05
1968S	–	–	.05
1969 P&D	–	–	.05
1969S	–	–	.10
Complete Collection Lincoln Cents–1934–1969S All Mints–Uncirculated. 95 Pieces without 1955 Double Die	–	–	75.00

26.
BRONZE TWO-CENT PIECES–
1864–1873

	Good	*Fine*	*Unc.*	*Proof*
1864 Small Motto	35.00	60.00	250.00	–
1864 Large Motto	2.00	4.00	20.00	175.00
1865	2.00	4.00	20.00	125.00
1866	2.25	5.00	30.00	110.00
1867	2.25	5.00	30.00	100.00
1868	2.25	5.00	30.00	100.00
1869	2.50	6.00	30.00	100.00
1870	3.50	8.00	40.00	100.00
1871	5.00	9.00	50.00	100.00
1872	30.00	50.00	120.00	200.00
1873	–	–	–	500.00

27.

NICKEL THREE-CENT PIECES—

1865–1889

	Good	*Fine*	*Unc.*	*Proof*
1865	1.25	2.00	15.00	400.00
1866	1.50	2.50	15.00	100.00
1867	1.50	2.50	15.00	60.00
1868	1.50	2.50	15.00	60.00
1869	1.75	3.00	17.50	60.00
1870	1.75	3.00	17.50	60.00
1871	2.25	4.00	20.00	60.00
1872	2.25	4.00	20.00	60.00
1873	1.75	2.50	20.00	40.00
1874	2.50	5.00	25.00	50.00
1875	5.00	9.00	35.00	52.50
1876	4.50	8.00	35.00	52.50
1877	—	—	—	500.00
1878	—	—	—	150.00
1879	5.00	6.00	30.00	37.50
1880	5.00	6.00	30.00	32.50
1881	1.75	2.50	15.00	25.00
1882	4.00	8.00	30.00	27.50
1883	4.00	8.00	30.00	27.50
1884	4.50	10.00	30.00	32.50
1885	4.50	10.00	30.00	32.50
1886	—	—	—	50.00
1887 87 over 86	—	—	—	160.00
1887	15.00	25.00	80.00	95.00
1888	5.00	10.00	30.00	30.00
1889	5.00	10.00	30.00	30.00

28.

NICKEL FIVE-CENT PIECES–1866–1883

SHIELD TYPE

1866–1867

1867–1883

	Good	*Fine*	*Unc.*	*Proof*
1866	5.00	10.00	100.00	1,000.00
1867 Rays	6.50	17.50	150.00	–
1867 Without Rays	2.00	3.00	25.00	60.00
1868	2.00	3.00	25.00	60.00
1869	2.50	5.00	30.00	65.00
1870	3.00	6.00	35.00	65.00
1871	30.00	50.00	175.00	250.00
1872	3.50	7.50	30.00	50.00
1873	3.50	7.50	30.00	40.00
1874	6.00	10.00	30.00	70.00
1875	11.00	20.00	90.00	140.00
1876	6.00	9.00	35.00	50.00
1877	–	–	–	800.00
1878	–	–	–	225.00
1879	12.00	20.00	50.00	70.00
1880	15.00	22.00	60.00	70.00
1881	11.00	17.50	50.00	70.00
1882	2.00	4.00	25.00	50.00
1883	2.50	5.00	25.00	50.00

LIBERTY HEAD TYPE

1883

1883–1912

	Good	*Fine*	*Unc.*	*Proof*
1883 Without CENTS	1.00	2.00	7.50	35.00
1883 With CENTS	3.75	7.50	22.00	40.00
1884	3.50	8.00	27.50	50.00
1885	50.00	85.00	200.00	295.00
1886	20.00	45.00	100.00	150.00
1887	2.00	4.50	24.00	40.00
1888	4.00	8.00	25.00	45.00
1889	2.00	4.00	22.00	35.00
1890	2.75	5.50	25.00	40.00
1891	1.75	3.75	27.50	40.00
1892	1.75	4.50	20.50	30.00
1893	1.75	4.00	20.50	30.00
1894	4.00	9.00	36.00	40.00
1895	1.50	4.50	31.50	40.00
1896	2.00	9.00	40.00	90.00
1897	1.25	3.50	20.00	45.00
1898	1.25	3.50	20.00	45.00
1899	1.00	3.00	20.00	45.00
1900	.60	2.50	16.00	40.00
1901	.50	2.25	14.50	40.00
1902	.50	2.25	14.00	40.00
1903	.50	2.25	12.00	40.00
1904	.50	2.25	12.00	40.00
1905	.50	2.25	13.50	40.00
1906	.50	2.25	12.50	40.00
1907	.50	2.25	12.50	40.00
1908	.50	2.25	12.00	35.00
1909	.50	2.25	12.00	35.00
1910	.50	2.25	12.00	35.00
1911	.50	2.25	11.00	37.00
1912	.50	2.25	11.00	50.00
1912D	1.50	9.50	175.00	–
1912S	25.00	45.00	350.00	–
1913 Liberty Head. 5 Known	46,000.00	–	–	–

INDIAN HEAD OR BUFFALO TYPE

1913

1913–1938

				Matte Proof
1913 Var. 1	.75	1.50	5.50	200.00
1913D Var. 1	2.00	3.50	20.00	–
1913S Var. 1	3.50	7.50	35.00	–
1913 Var. 2	.75	1.50	7.00	200.00
1913D Var. 2	12.50	22.50	60.00	–
1913S Var. 2	25.00	45.00	100.00	–
1914	1.00	2.75	15.00	200.00
1914D	11.00	22.50	100.00	–
1914S	2.50	8.50	60.00	–
1915	.85	2.25	15.00	200.00
1915D	2.50	7.50	55.00	–
1915S	7.00	15.00	100.00	–
1916	.35	1.25	9.00	300.00
1916D	1.50	4.50	45.00	–
1916S	1.75	5.50	47.50	–
1917	.35	.85	11.00	
1917D	2.50	8.50	70.00	–
1917S	2.75	9.00	100.00	–

	Good	*Fine*	*Unc.*
1918	.40	1.75	30.00
1918D over 7	1.50	325.00	4,000.00
1918D Normal date	2.75	8.50	150.00
1918S	2.50	8.50	150.00
1919	.30	1.00	20.00
1919D	2.75	10.00	175.00
1919S	2.75	11.50	175.00
1920	.30	.75	20.00
1920D	2.25	7.50	175.00
1920S	2.25	7.50	175.00
1921	.60	1.75	50.00
1921S	8.00	20.00	300.00
1923	.35	1.00	17.50
1923S	1.75	6.00	150.00
1924	.35	.90	20.00
1924D	1.75	5.00	150.00
1924S	5.00	15.00	500.00
1925	.30	.85	20.00
1925D	4.00	11.00	200.00
1925S	2.00	8.00	200.00

	Good	Fine	Unc.
1926	.25	.65	15.00
1926D	2.25	8.00	290.00
1926S	3.50	15.00	400.00
1927	.25	.60	14.00
1927D	.75	2.00	40.00
1927S	1.00	5.00	210.00
1928	.25	.50	15.00
1928D	.30	1.00	15.00
1928S	.50	1.50	50.00
1929	.30	.60	10.00
1929D	.25	.70	15.00
1929S	.25	.70	15.00
1930	.25	.70	12.00
1930S	.60	1.50	35.00
1931S	3.50	5.50	50.00
1934	.20	.60	10.00
1934D	.20	.40	10.00
1935	–	.40	5.00
1935D	–	.40	9.00
1935S	–	.30	7.00
1936	–	–	4.00
1936D	–	–	4.00
1936S	–	–	5.00
1937	–	–	4.00
1937D	–	–	4.00
1937D 3-Legged Var.	35.00	45.00	200.00
1937S	–	–	6.00
1938D	–	–	4.00

JEFFERSON TYPE

	–	Ex. Fine	Unc.
1938	–	–	2.00
1938D	–	2.75	5.00
1938S	–	3.90	6.00
1939	–	–	1.50
1939D	–	8.50	30.00
1939S	–	3.00	7.50
1940	–	–	1.00
1940D	–	–	1.25
1940S	–	–	1.75
1941	–	–	.80
1941D	–	–	1.00
1941S	–	–	1.50
1942	–	–	1.75
1942D	–	2.25	7.50

		Ex. Fine	Unc.
1942P Wartime Silver Nickels	–	–	6.00
1942S	–	–	4.00
1943P	–	.45	1.75
1943D	–	1.00	4.00
1943S	–	.65	1.50
1944P	–	.45	2.25
1944D	–	.45	3.00
1944S	–	.75	3.00
1945P	–	.60	3.00
1945D	–	.60	2.00
1945S	–	.60	1.75
1946 Regular Nickels	–	–	.40
1946D	–	–	.75
1946S	–	–	1.50
1947	–	–	.60
1947D	–	–	.75
1947S	–	–	1.25
1948	–	–	.50
1948D	–	–	.75
1948S	–	–	1.25
1949	–	–	1.00
1949D	–	–	1.25
1949S	–	–	2.50
1950	–	–	2.50
1950D	–	5.00	12.00

	Unc.
1951	1.00
1951D	1.50
1951S	5.00
1952	.50
1952D	3.00
1952S	1.00
1953	.50
1953D	.50
1953S	1.00
1954	.35
1954D	.35
1954S	.50
1955	2.25
1955D	.50
1956	.35
1956D	.30
1957	.35
1957D	.25
1958	.75
1958D	.25
1959	.30
1959D	.20
1960	.20
1960D	.20
1961	.25
1961D	.20
1962	.20
1962D	.20
1963P	.20
1963D	.15

	Unc.
1964	.15
1964D	.15
1965	.15
1966	.15
1967	.15
1968	.15
1968D	.15
1968S	.15
1969D&S ea.	.15
Complete Set Jefferson Nickels. 1939–1969S. All Mints. Uncirculated. 77 Pieces	152.00
Complete Set Wartime Nickels. 1942P–1945S. All Mints. Uncirculated. 11 pieces	32.00

29.

SILVER THREE-CENT PIECES–

1851–1873

	Good	Fine	Unc.	Proof
1851	4.00	9.00	40.00	–
1851O	8.50	25.00	100.00	–
1852	3.00	7.00	45.00	–
1853	3.00	7.00	40.00	–
1854	8.00	15.00	60.00	–
1855	12.00	30.00	150.00	850.00
1856	7.00	12.00	75.00	850.00
1857	7.00	12.00	75.00	800.00
1858	6.00	11.00	75.00	425.00
1859	10.00	15.00	45.00	125.00
1860	10.00	15.00	45.00	125.00
1861	8.00	13.00	40.00	125.00
1862	8.00	13.00	40.00	125.00
1863	–	–	150.00	200.00
1864	–	–	200.00	250.00
1865	–	–	–	210.00
1866	–	–	–	125.00
1867	–	–	–	125.00
1868	–	–	–	125.00
1869	–	–	–	125.00
1870	–	–	–	125.00
1871	–	–	–	125.00
1872	–	–	–	125.00
1873	–	–	–	225.00

30.
HALF DIMES–
1794–1873

FLOWING HAIR TYPE

	Good	Fine	Unc.
1794	200.00	400.00	1,500.00
1795	150.00	300.00	850.00
1796 over 5	300.00	500.00	1,500.00

DRAPED BUST TYPE

1796–1797

1800–1805

1796 Normal Date	150.00	300.00	1,200.00
1796 LIBERTY	200.00	400.00	–
1797 15 Stars	150.00	300.00	1,000.00
1797 16 Stars	150.00	300.00	1,000.00
1797 13 Stars	150.00	300.00	1,000.00
1800	100.00	250.00	900.00
1801	125.00	300.00	1,000.00
1802	1,000.00	3,000.00	–
1803	100.00	225.00	850.00
1805	175.00	400.00	1,000.00

LIBERTY CAP TYPE

	Good	Fine	Unc.
1829	5.00	10.00	60.00
1830	4.00	8.00	60.00
1831	4.00	8.00	60.00
1832	4.00	8.00	60.00
1833	4.00	8.00	60.00
1834	4.00	8.00	60.00
1835	4.00	8.00	60.00
1836	4.00	8.00	60.00
1837	4.00	8.00	60.00

LIBERTY SEATED TYPE

1837–1838

1838–1859

1860–1873

1837 No Stars	40.00	75.00	250.00
1838O No Stars	50.00	100.00	450.00
1838 No Drapery at Elbow	2.50	5.00	40.00
1839 No Drapery at Elbow	2.50	5.00	40.00
1839O No Drapery at Elbow	4.50	8.50	45.00
1840 No Drapery at Elbow	2.25	4.50	35.00
1840O No Drapery at Elbow	4.50	11.00	100.00
1840 Drapery at Elbow	2.25	5.00	50.00
1840O Drapery at Elbow	5.00	12.50	100.00
1841	2.00	4.50	35.00
1841O	3.00	7.50	100.00
1842	2.00	4.00	30.00
1842O	5.00	15.00	125.00
1843	2.50	4.00	30.00
1844	3.00	7.50	35.00
1844O	6.00	17.50	100.00
1845	2.00	3.50	30.00
1846	42.50	75.00	250.00
1847	2.00	4.00	30.00
1848	2.00	4.00	30.00
1848O	4.50	11.00	90.00
1849 over 48	2.50	5.75	40.00
1849 over 46	2.50	5.75	40.00
1849	2.00	4.00	30.00
1849O	22.50	55.00	200.00
1850	2.00	4.00	30.00

	Good	Fine	Unc.
1850O	3.00	7.50	80.00
1851	2.00	4.00	30.00
1851O	2.75	6.75	80.00
1852	2.00	4.00	30.00
1852O	4.50	15.00	120.00
1853 No Arrows	8.00	17.50	90.00
1853O No Arrows	57.50	110.00	500.00

	Good	Fine	Unc.	Proof
1853 With Arrows	2.50	4.50	40.00	–
1853O	2.50	4.50	45.00	–
1854	2.00	4.00	30.00	–
1854O	2.00	3.75	40.00	–
1855	2.00	4.00	30.00	400.00
1855O	3.00	7.00	80.00	–
1856 No Arrows	2.00	3.00	30.00	325.00
1856O	2.00	4.00	35.00	–
1857	2.00	3.00	35.00	325.00
1857O	2.00	3.50	35.00	–
1858	2.00	3.00	30.00	325.00
1858O	2.00	3.75	35.00	–
1859	3.00	6.00	35.00	125.00
1859O	3.00	6.00	45.00	–
1860	2.00	4.00	35.00	75.00
1860O	2.75	5.00	30.00	–
1861	2.00	3.00	30.00	75.00
1862	2.00	3.00	30.00	75.00
1863	8.50	16.00	90.00	125.00
1863S	8.50	16.00	75.00	–
1864	–	–	–	250.00
1864S	9.50	22.50	100.00	–
1865	8.00	14.00	90.00	150.00
1865S	6.50	14.00	75.00	–
1866	6.50	14.00	75.00	125.00
1866S	5.00	9.00	70.00	–
1867	6.50	14.00	75.00	125.00
1867S	4.25	8.50	70.00	–
1868	2.50	5.00	35.00	75.00
1868S	2.50	5.00	35.00	–
1869	2.50	5.00	30.00	75.00
1869S	2.50	5.00	30.00	–
1870	2.00	4.00	30.00	50.00
1871	2.00	4.00	30.00	50.00
1871S	9.00	20.00	75.00	–
1872	2.00	4.00	30.00	60.00
1872S Mint Mark within Wreath	2.00	4.00	40.00	–
1872S Mint Mark below Wreath	2.00	4.00	40.00	–
1873	2.00	3.00	30.00	100.00
1873S	2.00	5.00	35.00	–

31.

DIMES–
1796–Date

DRAPED BUST TYPE

1796–1797

1798–1807

	Good	Fine	Unc.
1796	300.00	700.00	2,000.00
1797 16 Stars	260.00	600.00	1,800.00
1797 13 Stars	250.00	550.00	1,800.00
1798 over 97, 13 Stars on Reverse	–	500.00	–
1798 over 97, 16 Stars on Reverse	125.00	300.00	950.00
1798	125.00	300.00	950.00
1800	100.00	200.00	700.00
1801	125.00	300.00	800.00
1802	150.00	350.00	1,000.00
1803	125.00	300.00	900.00
1804 13 Stars on Reverse	150.00	300.00	1,250.00
1804 14 Stars on Reverse	150.00	300.00	1,250.00
1805	100.00	150.00	500.00
1807	100.00	150.00	500.00

LIBERTY CAP TYPE

	Good	Fine	Unc.
1809	50.00	100.00	400.00
1811 over 9	35.00	60.00	250.00

	Good	Fine	Unc.
1814	15.00	25.00	150.00
1820	15.00	25.00	150.00
1821	7.50	20.00	125.00
1822	45.00	100.00	550.00
1823 over 22	10.00	25.00	150.00
1824 over 22	10.00	25.00	200.00
1825	10.00	20.00	150.00
1827	10.00	20.00	150.00
1828	12.00	25.00	175.00
1829	5.00	15.00	100.00
1830	5.00	15.00	100.00
1831	4.50	9.00	100.00
1832	4.50	9.00	100.00
1833	4.50	9.00	100.00
1834	4.50	9.00	100.00
1835	4.50	9.00	100.00
1836	4.50	9.00	100.00
1837	4.50	9.00	100.00

LIBERTY SEATED TYPE

No Stars

Stars

	Good	Fine	Unc.
1837 No Stars	40.00	90.00	325.00
1838O No Stars	50.00	115.00	500.00
1838 With Stars	5.00	7.50	75.00
1838 With Partial Drapery	12.50	30.00	100.00
1839	2.75	5.50	50.00
1839O	4.00	10.00	50.00
1840	2.75	6.00	45.00
1840O	4.00	8.00	45.00
1841	2.00	4.00	40.00
1841O	2.00	5.00	50.00

	Good	Fine	Unc.	Proof
1842	2.00	4.00	35.00	–
1842O	4.00	7.50	50.00	–
1843	2.00	4.00	35.00	–
1843O	12.50	30.00	200.00	–
1844	17.50	50.00	250.00	–
1845	2.00	4.00	35.00	–
1845O	6.50	12.50	70.00	–
1846	12.50	25.00	150.00	–
1847	4.00	7.50	50.00	–
1848	3.00	5.50	35.00	–
1849	2.00	4.00	35.00	–
1849O	5.50	15.00	100.00	–
1850	2.00	4.00	35.00	–
1850O	4.50	11.00	55.00	–
1851	2.00	4.00	40.00	–
1851O	4.00	7.50	55.00	–

	Good	Fine	Unc.	Proof
1852	2.00	4.00	35.00	–
1852O	4.00	9.00	60.00	–
1853 (No Arrows)	15.00	25.00	125.00	–
1853 With Arrows	2.25	4.50	50.00	–
1853O	4.00	6.50	45.00	–
1854	2.00	4.00	40.00	–
1854O	2.25	4.00	40.00	–
1855	2.00	4.00	40.00	400.00
1856	2.00	4.00	40.00	400.00
1856O	2.75	5.00	45.00	–
1856S	25.00	60.00	250.00	–
1857	2.00	4.00	40.00	325.00
1857O	2.25	4.50	40.00	–
1858	1.25	3.50	40.00	275.00
1858O	3.50	7.50	40.00	–
1858S	15.00	35.00	200.00	–
1859	1.75	3.50	35.00	150.00
1859O	1.75	4.00	40.00	–
1859S	15.00	25.00	125.00	–
1860S	7.50	22.50	100.00	–

1860–1891

1860	1.75	4.00	35.00	80.00
1860O	60.00	135.00	750.00	–
1861	1.50	3.00	35.00	80.00
1861S	10.00	27.50	125.00	–
1862	2.25	4.00	35.00	80.00
1862S	7.50	20.00	100.00	–
1863	10.00	20.00	85.00	100.00
1863S	7.50	20.00	125.00	–
1864	10.00	20.00	85.00	125.00
1864S	8.00	15.00	50.00	–
1865	12.00	24.00	90.00	100.00
1865S	8.50	20.00	100.00	–
1866	10.00	20.00	90.00	100.00
1866S	7.50	17.50	100.00	–
1867	10.00	20.00	100.00	100.00
1867S	7.50	16.50	90.00	–
1868	1.75	3.50	35.00	90.00
1868S	5.00	10.00	60.00	–
1869	2.00	4.00	35.00	90.00
1869S	5.00	11.50	50.00	–
1870	1.75	3.50	35.00	70.00
1870S	37.50	75.00	275.00	–
1871	1.75	4.00	35.00	70.00
1871CC	120.00	250.00	1,500.00	–
1871S	8.50	20.00	125.00	–
1872	1.50	4.00	35.00	70.00

	Good	Fine	Unc.	Proof
1872CC	80.00	160.00	800.00	–
1872S	8.50	17.50	90.00	–
1873	1.50	5.00	35.00	70.00
1873CC (Unique)	–	–	–	–
1873 Arrows at date	9.00	17.00	150.00	250.00
1873CC	300.00	575.00	1,400.00	–
1873S	12.50	25.00	150.00	–
1874	9.00	17.00	150.00	250.00
1874CC	70.00	175.00	1,750.00	–
1874S	15.00	30.00	175.00	–
1875 Arrows at Date Removed	1.50	3.00	30.00	60.00
1875CC Under Wreath	3.00	6.50	40.00	–
1875CC In Wreath	1.75	3.50	40.00	–
1875S Under Wreath	1.50	3.00	30.00	–
1875S In Wreath	1.50	3.00	30.00	–
1876	1.25	2.50	30.00	60.00
1876CC	1.75	3.50	35.00	–
1876S	1.50	3.25	30.00	–
1877	1.00	2.00	30.00	125.00
1877CC	1.50	2.50	30.00	–
1877S	1.50	2.50	30.00	–
1878	1.50	2.50	30.00	60.00
1878CC	11.00	23.50	90.00	–
1879	10.00	20.00	65.00	70.00
1880	9.00	15.00	60.00	65.00
1881	9.00	15.00	60.00	65.00
1882	1.00	2.00	30.00	60.00
1883	1.00	2.00	30.00	60.00
1884	1.00	2.00	30.00	60.00
1884S	7.00	13.00	70.00	–
1885	1.00	2.00	30.00	60.00
1885S	55.00	100.00	450.00	–
1886	1.00	2.50	30.00	60.00
1886S	7.00	14.00	60.00	–
1887	1.00	2.50	30.00	60.00
1887S	2.00	4.00	30.00	–
1888	1.00	2.50	30.00	60.00
1888S	2.75	5.00	35.00	–
1889	1.00	2.50	30.00	60.00
1889S	7.50	15.00	125.00	–
1890	1.00	2.50	30.00	65.00
1890S	2.75	5.00	35.00	–
1891	1.00	2.50	30.00	65.00
1891O	2.25	4.50	40.00	–
1891S	1.75	3.25	35.00	–

BARBER OR LIBERTY HEAD TYPE

	Good	Fine	Unc.	Proof
1892	.75	2.25	20.00	60.00
1892O	1.75	4.00	30.00	—
1892S	15.00	25.00	90.00	—
1893	1.75	3.50	20.00	65.00
1893O	4.00	9.00	45.00	—
1893S	4.00	9.00	45.00	—
1894	3.50	6.00	25.00	65.00
1894O	20.00	60.00	260.00	—
1894S (Very rare)	—	—	—	12,250.00
1895	20.00	40.00	140.00	200.00
1895O	45.00	120.00	600.00	—
1895S	6.00	12.00	95.00	—
1896	2.50	6.00	22.50	80.00
1896O	17.50	42.50	170.00	—
1896S	25.00	50.00	225.00	—
1897	.75	2.25	20.00	80.00
1897O	17.50	35.00	185.00	—
1897S	5.00	15.00	90.00	—
1898	.50	1.50	17.00	70.00
1898O	2.50	7.50	100.00	—
1898S	3.00	7.50	65.00	—
1899	.50	1.50	20.00	25.00
1899O	3.00	9.00	90.00	—
1899S	2.75	7.50	60.00	—
1900	.40	1.50	20.00	70.00
1900O	2.75	8.00	85.00	—
1900S	1.50	5.00	50.00	—
1901	.40	1.50	20.00	75.00
1901O	1.00	6.00	80.00	—
1901S	17.50	70.00	450.00	—
1902	.40	1.00	17.00	75.00
1902O	1.00	5.00	55.00	—
1902S	3.00	8.00	70.00	—
1903	.35	1.00	20.00	75.00
1903O	.75	5.00	45.00	—
1903S	10.00	20.00	150.00	—
1904	.30	1.00	20.00	80.00
1904S	9.00	18.00	100.00	—
1905	.35	1.00	20.00	80.00
1905O	1.25	4.00	50.00	—
1905S	.35	1.00	75.00	—
1906	.35	1.00	20.00	75.00
1906D	1.00	2.50	20.00	—
1906O	1.00	4.00	30.00	—
1906S	1.00	3.25	25.00	—
1907	.35	1.00	20.00	80.00
1907D	.90	3.00	30.00	—
1907O	.65	2.00	25.00	—
1907S	1.25	3.00	25.00	—
1908	.30	1.00	20.00	80.00
1908D	.40	1.25	20.00	—
1908O	2.00	4.00	35.00	—
1908S	1.00	3.25	30.00	—
1909	.30	1.00	30.00	75.00
1909D	2.00	8.00	45.00	—
1909O	1.75	9.00	50.00	—
1909S	2.00	8.50	50.00	—

	Good	Fine	Unc.	Proof
1910	.25	1.00	20.00	80.00
1910D	.50	1.75	20.00	—
1910S	1.75	4.00	37.50	—
1911	.25	1.00	20.00	80.00
1911D	.40	1.25	20.00	—
1911S	.25	2.50	25.00	—
1912	.25	1.00	20.00	85.00
1912D	.35	1.25	20.00	—
1912S	1.00	3.00	30.00	—
1913	.25	1.00	20.00	125.00
1913S	7.00	25.00	175.00	—
1914	.25	1.00	20.00	200.00
1914D	.35	1.25	20.00	—
1914S	1.00	3.00	35.00	—
1915	.25	1.25	20.00	200.00
1915S	1.50	4.00	30.00	—
1916	.25	1.00	20.00	—
1916S	.30	1.50	20.00	—

MERCURY TYPE

	Good	Fine	Unc.
1916	.30	.80	8.00
1916D	85.00	180.00	650.00
1916S	1.25	3.00	17.50
1917	.25	.50	8.00
1917D	1.00	4.00	60.00
1917S	.35	1.25	20.00
1918	.40	1.25	22.50
1918D	.40	2.25	35.00
1918S	.50	2.00	30.00
1919	.30	1.25	27.50
1919D	1.00	4.50	100.00
1919S	1.00	4.50	100.00
1920	.25	.50	10.00
1920D	.40	1.75	37.50

	Good	Fine	Ex. Fine	Unc.
1920S	—	1.50	8.00	30.00
1921	10.00	35.00	100.00	350.00
1921D	15.00	45.00	100.00	300.00
1923	—	.75	1.75	12.00
1923S	.75	3.00	15.00	75.00
1924	—	.75	3.00	20.00
1924D	—	2.00	10.00	85.00
1924S	—	2.00	12.00	80.00
1925	—	.75	2.50	20.00
1925D	1.50	8.00	70.00	300.00

	Good	Fine	Ex. Fine	Unc.
1925S	–	2.25	15.00	90.00
1926	–	.75	3.00	15.00
1926D	–	1.50	10.00	45.00
1926S	5.00	10.00	55.00	300.00
1927	–	.60	2.00	12.00
1927D	–	3.00	30.00	175.00
1927S	–	2.00	17.50	100.00
1928	–	.50	2.00	12.00
1928D	–	3.00	25.00	100.00
1928S	–	1.50	12.00	50.00
1929	–	.50	1.50	7.50
1929D	–	1.50	4.00	15.00
1929S	–	1.50	4.00	20.00
1930	–	1.00	4.00	15.00
1930S	1.25	4.00	15.00	50.00
1931	–	2.00	5.00	30.00
1931D	4.00	8.00	20.00	60.00
1931S	2.50	4.00	15.00	50.00
1934	–	.35	1.25	7.50
1934D	–	.75	3.00	15.00
1935	–	.35	.70	3.50
1935D	–	.60	2.50	20.00
1935S	–	.50	1.25	8.00
1936	–	–	–	2.50
1936D	–	–	2.00	15.00
1936S	–	–	2.00	10.00
1937	–	–	–	2.00
1937D	–	–	1.00	6.00
1937S	–	–	1.00	7.00
1938	–	–	–	3.00
1938D	–	–	1.50	9.00
1938S	–	–	1.50	5.50
1939	–	–	–	2.00
1939D	–	–	–	3.00
1939S	–	–	1.50	9.00
1940	–	–	–	2.00
1940D	–	–	–	2.00
1940S	–	–	–	2.00
1941	–	–	–	1.50
1941D	–	–	–	2.00
1941S	–	–	–	2.00
1942 over 41	70.00	120.00	190.00	500.00
1942	–	–	–	1.25
1942D	–	–	–	1.50
1942S	–	–	–	2.00
1943	–	–	–	1.25
1943D	–	–	–	1.75
1943S	–	–	–	1.75
1944	–	–	–	1.50
1944D	–	–	–	1.50
1944S	–	–	–	1.50
1945	–	–	–	1.50
1945D	–	–	–	1.50
1945S	–	–	–	1.50

ROOSEVELT TYPE

	Unc.
1946	.50
1946D	.50
1946S	1.25
1947	1.00
1947D	1.25
1947S	1.00
1948	2.00
1948D	1.00
1948S	1.00
1949	8.00
1949D	2.00
1949S	12.50
1950	1.50
1950D	1.50
1950S	9.00
1951	1.00
1951D	1.00
1951S	7.50
1952	1.00
1952D	.50
1952S	2.00
1953	.75
1953D	.50
1953S	1.00
1954	.50
1954D	.50
1954S	1.00
1955	2.00
1955D	1.50
1955S	1.00
1956	.25
1956D	.35
1957	.25
1957D	.50
1958	.75
1958D	.35
1959	.25
1959D	.30
1960	.30
1960D	.30
1961	.30
1961D	.30
1962	.30
1962D	.30

	Unc.
1963	.30
1963D	.30
1964	.25
1964D	.25
1965	.20
1966	.20
1967	.20
1968	.20
1968D	.20
1969	.20
1969D	.20
1969S	.20
Complete Collection Roosevelt Dimes. 1946–1969D All Mints. Uncirculated 59 Pieces	79.00

32.
TWENTY-CENT PIECES–
1875–1878

	Good	*Fine*	*V. Fine*	*Unc.*	*Proof*
1875	20.00	40.00	50.00	175.00	225.00
1875CC	25.00	45.00	55.00	190.00	–
1875S	20.00	40.00	50.00	160.00	–
1876	27.50	45.00	60.00	180.00	225.00
1876CC (14 known)	–	–	–	–	12,750.00
1877	–	–	–	–	600.00
1878	–	–	–	–	400.00

33. QUARTER-DOLLARS– 1796–Date

DRAPED BUST TYPE

1796

1804–1807

	Good	Fine	Unc.
1796	700.00	2,000.00	5,000.00
1804	150.00	350.00	–
1805	60.00	125.00	800.00
1806 over 5	50.00	125.00	800.00
1806	40.00	100.00	700.00
1807	40.00	125.00	800.00

LIBERTY HEAD TYPE

1815–1828

1831–1838

1815	15.00	40.00	500.00
1818 over 15	20.00	50.00	450.00
1818	15.00	40.00	375.00
1819	15.00	40.00	375.00
1820	15.00	40.00	375.00

	Good	Fine	Unc.
1821	15.00	40.00	375.00
1822	20.00	45.00	400.00
1822 25 over 50c	150.00	300.00	1,500.00
1823 over 22	600.00	1,200.00	–
1824	30.00	60.00	400.00
1825 over 22	20.00	35.00	350.00
1825 over 23	20.00	35.00	350.00
1825 over 24	20.00	35.00	350.00
1827 6 or 7 known (rare)	–	–	–
1828	20.00	35.00	350.00
1828 25 over 50c	60.00	125.00	600.00
1831	12.00	20.00	250.00
1832	12.00	20.00	250.00
1833	12.00	20.00	250.00
1834	12.00	20.00	250.00
1835	12.00	20.00	250.00
1836	12.00	20.00	250.00
1837	12.00	20.00	250.00
1838	12.00	20.00	250.00

LIBERTY SEATED TYPE

1838–1865

1866–1891

1838 No Drapery	6.00	15.00	100.00
1839 No Drapery	5.00	14.00	100.00
1840O No Drapery	5.00	13.00	100.00
1840 Drapery	5.50	13.00	100.00
1840O Drapery	5.00	13.00	100.00
1841	12.50	22.50	125.00
1841O	4.00	9.00	90.00
1842	4.00	9.00	60.00
1842O	4.50	10.00	70.00
1843	3.50	7.50	50.00
1843O	3.50	7.50	60.00
1844	3.50	7.50	60.00
1844O	4.00	6.00	60.00
1845	3.25	7.00	60.00
1846	3.50	7.50	60.00
1847	3.50	7.00	500.00
1847O	4.00	8.00	60.00
1848	4.00	8.00	60.00
1849	3.25	7.00	60.00
1849O	60.00	125.00	600.00
1850	4.00	8.50	60.00
1850O	4.00	8.00	60.00
1851	4.00	8.00	60.00
1851O	4.00	9.00	80.00
1852	4.00	9.00	60.00

	Good	Fine	Unc.
1852O	6.50	13.00	70.00
1853 over 52. No Arrows or Rays	45.00	100.00	400.00

	Good	Fine	Unc.	Proof
1853 Arrows and Rays	5.00	10.00	200.00	–
1853O	8.00	15.00	200.00	–
1854 Arrows, no Rays	3.50	6.00	60.00	–
1854O	3.50	6.00	60.00	–
1855	3.50	6.00	60.00	550.00
1855O	35.00	70.00	350.00	–
1855S	40.00	75.00	375.00	–
1856 No Arrows	2.75	4.00	40.00	475.00
1856O	3.00	6.00	35.00	–
1856S	15.00	37.00	200.00	–
1857	2.50	4.00	40.00	475.00
1857O	3.00	5.00	35.00	–
1857S	15.00	32.50	210.00	–
1858	3.00	5.00	35.00	350.00
1858O	4.00	6.50	40.00	–
1858S	25.00	37.50	225.00	–
1859	3.00	4.50	40.00	140.00
1859O	3.50	5.50	40.00	–
1859S	25.00	37.50	225.00	–
1860	2.50	4.50	30.00	110.00
1860O	3.00	5.00	40.00	–
1860S	15.00	30.00	225.00	–
1861	2.50	4.50	30.00	110.00
1861S	14.50	25.00	200.00	–
1862	2.50	4.00	40.00	110.00
1862S	14.00	20.00	200.00	–
1863	3.25	6.00	40.00	110.00
1864	4.00	8.00	45.00	110.00
1864S	20.00	45.00	275.00	–
1865	4.00	8.00	45.00	110.00
1865S	9.00	17.00	160.00	–
1866	4.00	6.50	55.00	100.00
1866S	10.00	20.00	175.00	–
1867	3.25	7.00	50.00	95.00
1867S	10.00	17.00	150.00	–
1868	4.00	6.50	50.00	95.00
1868S	9.00	14.00	125.00	–
1869	4.00	8.00	60.00	95.00
1869S	9.00	14.00	125.00	–
1870	3.00	4.50	45.00	95.00
1870CC	120.00	175.00	900.00	–
1871	2.50	3.50	40.00	90.00
1871CC	100.00	150.00	800.00	–
1871S	7.50	17.50	130.00	–
1872	2.50	4.00	40.00	90.00
1872CC	150.00	250.00	1,200.00	–
1872S	15.00	25.00	125.00	–
1873 No Arrows	6.00	12.00	60.00	95.00
1873CC	350.00	650.00	–	–
1873 Arrows	15.00	25.00	175.00	300.00
1873CC	300.00	550.00	1,700.00	–
1873S	20.00	35.00	200.00	–
1874	15.00	25.00	175.00	250.00

	Good	Fine	Unc.	Proof
1874S	22.50	35.00	225.00	–
1875	2.50	3.75	35.00	75.00
1875CC	9.00	15.00	125.00	–
1875S	9.00	15.00	100.00	–
1876	2.50	3.75	35.00	65.00
1876CC	3.00	5.00	40.00	–
1876S	2.50	4.25	35.00	–
1877	2.50	4.00	35.00	100.00
1877CC	3.00	5.00	30.00	–
1877S	2.50	4.00	35.00	–
1878	2.50	4.25	35.00	65.00
1878CC	5.00	9.00	60.00	–
1878S	125.00	250.00	900.00	–
1879	17.50	30.00	65.00	110.00
1880	15.00	25.00	65.00	80.00
1881	15.00	25.00	65.00	80.00
1882	15.00	25.00	65.00	80.00
1883	15.00	25.00	65.00	80.00
1884	20.00	30.00	75.00	85.00
1885	15.00	25.00	65.00	85.00
1886	25.00	35.00	110.00	140.00
1887	20.00	30.00	75.00	80.00
1888	20.00	30.00	75.00	80.00
1888S	2.50	4.00	40.00	–
1889	15.00	25.00	65.00	85.00
1890	4.00	9.00	40.00	85.00
1891	2.50	4.50	40.00	85.00
1891O	75.00	100.00	500.00	–
1891S	2.50	4.75	40.00	–

BARBER OR LIBERTY HEAD TYPE

	Good	Fine	Ex. Fine	Unc.	Proof
1892	.90	2.25	8.00	30.00	80.00
1892O	3.00	6.50	15.00	40.00	–
1892S	9.00	20.00	50.00	135.00	–
1893	.90	2.00	10.00	35.00	80.00
1893O	1.75	5.00	15.00	40.00	–
1893S	2.75	7.50	16.00	50.00	–
1894	.90	2.25	10.00	40.00	80.00
1894O	1.75	5.00	15.00	50.00	–
1894S	1.75	5.00	14.00	50.00	–
1895	.85	2.00	10.00	35.00	80.00
1895O	1.50	6.50	30.00	95.00	–
1895S	2.50	7.00	15.00	65.00	–
1896	1.00	2.50	10.00	35.00	85.00

	Good	Fine	Ex. Fine	Unc.	Proof
1896O	3.50	10.00	55.00	200.00	—
1896S	75.00	175.00	450.00	1,250.00	—
1897	.75	2.00	10.00	35.00	85.00
1897O	6.00	14.00	45.00	125.00	—
1897S	7.50	17.50	45.00	150.00	—
1898	.75	2.00	10.00	40.00	85.00
1898O	1.75	5.00	25.00	90.00	—
1898S	2.00	7.00	25.00	100.00	—
1899	.75	1.75	10.00	35.00	80.00
1899O	1.50	5.00	20.00	75.00	—
1899S	5.50	10.00	25.00	90.00	—
1900	.65	1.75	10.00	35.00	80.00
1900O	2.00	6.00	20.00	75.00	—
1900S	1.25	6.50	35.00	87.50	—
1901	.60	1.75	10.00	35.00	80.00
1901O	7.50	25.00	95.00	300.00	—
1901S	200.00	400.00	750.00	1,750.00	—
1902	.60	1.75	10.00	35.00	85.00
1902O	1.75	7.50	20.00	70.00	—
1902S	2.50	9.50	35.00	100.00	—
1903	.60	1.75	10.00	35.00	85.00
1903O	2.00	8.00	50.00	150.00	—
1903S	3.00	10.00	50.00	150.00	—
1904	.60	1.75	10.00	35.00	90.00
1904O	4.00	14.00	55.00	250.00	—
1905	.75	2.00	10.00	40.00	90.00
1905O	4.50	12.50	40.00	150.00	—
1905S	2.50	7.00	25.00	80.00	—
1906	.75	2.00	10.00	35.00	90.00
1906D	1.25	3.00	10.00	40.00	—
1906O	1.50	4.00	15.00	45.00	—
1907	.60	2.00	3.50	30.00	95.00
1907D	1.25	3.00	10.00	40.00	—
1907O	1.00	3.00	10.00	40.00	—
1907S	1.75	5.00	20.00	60.00	—
1908	.60	2.00	10.00	35.00	95.00
1908D	.60	2.00	10.00	40.00	—
1908O	.60	2.00	10.00	40.00	—
1908S	4.00	10.00	25.00	75.00	—
1909	.50	1.75	10.00	40.00	95.00
1909D	.60	2.00	10.00	40.00	—
1909O	10.00	32.50	90.00	330.00	—
1909S	1.50	5.00	15.00	60.00	—
1910	.75	3.00	10.00	35.00	90.00
1910D	1.50	3.50	10.00	40.00	—
1911	.50	1.75	10.00	40.00	95.00
1911D	2.00	5.00	15.00	55.00	—
1911S	1.50	5.00	15.00	60.00	—
1912	.50	1.75	10.00	35.00	95.00
1912S	2.00	8.00	30.00	110.00	—
1913	3.00	7.50	25.00	90.00	140.00
1913D	1.25	4.00	10.00	50.00	—
1913S	90.00	195.00	500.00	1,000.00	—
1914	.50	1.75	10.00	40.00	240.00
1914D	.50	1.75	10.00	40.00	—
1914S	7.00	16.00	80.00	285.00	—
1915	.50	2.00	10.00	40.00	240.00

	Good	Fine	Ex. Fine	Unc.	Proof
1915D	.50	1.75	10.00	40.00	–
1915S	2.00	5.00	15.00	50.00	–
1916	.50	2.50	10.00	40.00	–
1916D	.50	2.00	10.00	40.00	–

STANDING LIBERTY TYPE

1916–1917

1917–1930

	Good	Fine	Ex. Fine	Unc.
1916	225.00	400.00	600.00	900.00
1917 Type 1	2.50	4.50	10.00	40.00
1917D	4.00	10.00	20.00	55.00
1917S	4.00	10.00	20.00	60.00
1917 Type 2	3.00	7.00	15.00	35.00
1917D	6.00	15.00	30.00	70.00
1917S	9.00	17.00	30.00	70.00
1918	3.00	10.00	25.00	50.00
1918D	7.00	15.00	30.00	80.00
1918S	3.00	10.00	20.00	60.00
1918S over 7	125.00	275.00	800.00	3,000.00
1919	4.00	9.00	24.00	55.00
1919D	20.00	40.00	100.00	275.00
1919S	25.00	50.00	100.00	325.00
1920	3.00	5.00	10.00	30.00
1920D	10.00	20.00	50.00	125.00
1920S	6.00	12.00	25.00	70.00
1921	20.00	40.00	90.00	250.00
1923	2.00	5.00	10.00	30.00
1923S	35.00	60.00	100.00	250.00
1924	2.50	5.00	10.00	35.00
1924D	8.00	12.00	20.00	50.00
1924S	10.00	20.00	30.00	100.00
1925	–	2.75	6.00	30.00
1926	–	2.75	6.00	30.00
1926D	–	3.00	7.50	30.00
1926S	–	6.50	40.00	150.00
1927	–	2.50	5.00	30.00
1927D	–	5.00	15.00	70.00
1927S	–	15.00	125.00	700.00
1928	–	2.00	6.00	30.00
1928D	–	2.00	6.00	30.00
1928S	–	2.00	6.00	30.00
1929	–	–	6.00	30.00
1929D	–	–	6.00	35.00
1929S	–	–	6.00	30.00
1930	–	–	6.00	25.00
1930S	–	–	6.00	35.00

WASHINGTON HEAD TYPE

	V.G.	Fine	Ex. Fine	Unc.
1932	—	—	3.00	15.00
1932D	35.00	45.00	70.00	200.00
1932S	35.00	45.00	70.00	100.00
1934	—	—	2.90	12.00
1934D	—	—	12.00	60.00
1935	—	—	2.50	9.00
1935D	—	—	9.00	55.00
1935S	—	—	8.00	35.00
1936	—	—	1.45	7.00
1936D	1.50	4.00	40.00	225.00
1936S	—	—	7.00	35.00
1937	—	—	1.75	7.00
1937D	—	—	3.00	11.00
1937S	—	—	17.00	50.00
1938	—	—	10.00	45.00
1938S	—	—	8.00	27.50
1939	—	—	2.00	6.00
1939D	—	—	2.50	9.00
1939S	—	—	8.00	30.00
1940	—	—	2.25	7.00
1940D	—	—	10.00	40.00
1940S	—	—	—	6.00
1941	—	—	—	2.00
1941D	—	—	—	5.00
1941S	—	—	—	5.00
1942	—	—	—	2.00
1942D	—	—	—	3.00
1942S	—	—	—	16.00
1943	—	—	—	1.75
1943D	—	—	—	3.00
1943S	—	—	—	4.50
1944	—	—	—	1.25
1944D	—	—	—	2.50
1944S	—	—	—	2.50
1945	—	—	—	1.00
1945D	—	—	—	3.00
1945S	—	—	—	2.50
1946	—	—	—	1.00
1946D	—	—	—	3.00
1946S	—	—	—	4.50

	V.G.	Fine	Ex. Fine	Unc.
1947	–	–	–	1.50
1947D	–	–	–	1.50
1947S	–	–	–	4.00
1948	–	–	–	1.10
1948D	–	–	–	2.00
1948S	–	–	–	2.00
1949	–	–	–	9.00
1949D	–	–	–	4.00
1950	–	–	–	1.00
1950D	–	–	–	1.50
1950S	–	–	–	3.00
1951	–	–	–	1.00
1951D	–	–	–	1.00
1951S	–	–	–	6.00
1952	–	–	–	1.00
1952D	–	–	–	1.00
1952S	–	–	–	3.00
1953	–	–	–	1.50
1953D	–	–	–	1.00
1953S	–	–	–	1.50
1954	–	–	–	.75
1954D	–	–	–	.75
1954S	–	–	–	1.50
1955	–	–	–	2.00
1955D	–	–	–	5.00
1956	–	–	–	.75
1956D	–	–	–	.75
1957	–	–	–	.75
1957D	–	–	–	.75
1958	–	–	–	2.00
1958D	–	–	–	.75
1959	–	–	–	.75
1959D	–	–	–	.70
1960	–	–	–	.70
1960D	–	–	–	.70
1961	–	–	–	.70
1961D	–	–	–	.70
1962	–	–	–	.70
1962D	–	–	–	.70
1963	–	–	–	.70
1963D	–	–	–	.70
1964	–	–	–	.70
1964D	–	–	–	.70
1965	–	–	–	.50
1966	–	–	–	.50
1967	–	–	–	.50
1968	–	–	–	.50
1968D	–	–	–	.50
1969PDS each	–	–	–	.50
Complete Collection Washington Quarters. 1932–1969D. All Mints. Uncirculated. 94 Pieces	–	–	–	1,132.00

HALF DOLLARS–
1794–Date

FLOWING HAIR TYPE

	Good	*Fine*	*V. Fine*	*Unc.*
1794	200.00	500.00	900.00	–
1795	125.00	250.00	500.00	–

DRAPED BUST TYPE

1796–1797

1801–1807

1796 15 Stars	1,200.00	3,000.00	4,000.00	–
1796 16 Stars	1,400.00	3,500.00	4,200.00	–
1797	1,200.00	3,000.00	4,000.00	–
1801	75.00	200.00	350.00	1,000.00
1802	60.00	175.00	300.00	850.00

	Good	Fine	V. Fine	Unc.
1803	40.00	75.00	150.00	550.00
1805 over 4	50.00	120.00	200.00	550.00
1805	25.00	50.00	100.00	450.00
1806 over 5	40.00	60.00	125.00	500.00
1806 over inverted 6	52.50	125.00	250.00	600.00
1806	25.00	50.00	100.00	350.00
1807	25.00	50.00	100.00	350.00

TURBAN HEAD TYPE

1807–1836 1836–1839

1807	17.00	35.00	75.00	400.00
1807 50 over 20	15.00	30.00	60.00	300.00
1808 over 7	10.00	25.00	40.00	150.00
1808	9.00	15.00	25.00	125.00
1809	9.00	15.00	25.00	125.00
1810	9.00	15.00	25.00	110.00
1811	7.00	12.00	25.00	125.00
1812 over 11	12.50	30.00	60.00	200.00
1812	8.00	14.00	25.00	110.00
1813	8.00	14.00	25.00	110.00
1814 over 13	10.00	30.00	40.00	175.00
1814	8.00	14.00	20.00	100.00
1815 over 12	85.00	150.00	200.00	800.00
1817 over 13	14.00	35.00	50.00	200.00
1817	6.00	14.00	20.00	90.00
1818 over 17	6.00	12.00	20.00	100.00
1818	6.00	14.00	20.00	70.00
1819 over 18	8.00	15.00	20.00	85.00
1819	6.00	14.00	20.00	80.00
1820 over 19	12.00	22.00	30.00	125.00
1820	12.00	25.00	30.00	130.00
1821	6.00	12.00	17.00	75.00
1822	6.00	12.00	17.00	75.00
1822 over 1	30.00	65.00	70.00	250.00
1823 Broken 3	15.00	30.00	40.00	125.00
1823	7.00	12.00	17.00	65.00
1824 over 21	10.00	20.00	30.00	90.00
1824 over Various Dates	8.00	15.00	20.00	75.00
1824	7.00	14.00	17.00	55.00
1825	7.00	14.00	17.00	55.00
1826	7.00	14.00	17.00	55.00
1827 over 6	10.00	20.00	35.00	125.00

	Good	Fine	V. Fine	Unc.
1827	5.00	7.00	11.00	50.00
1828	7.00	12.00	15.00	60.00
1829 over 21	8.00	14.00	20.00	70.00
1829	6.00	10.00	15.00	50.00
1830	5.00	10.00	14.00	50.00
1831	5.00	10.00	14.00	50.00
1832	5.00	10.00	14.00	50.00
1833	5.00	10.00	14.00	50.00
1834	5.00	10.00	14.00	45.00
1835	5.00	10.00	14.00	45.00
1836 (Lettered edge)	5.00	10.00	14.00	45.00
1836 50 over 00	25.00	45.00	60.00	200.00
1836 Reeded edge	45.00	75.00	130.00	300.00
1837	10.00	25.00	40.00	175.00
1838	10.00	25.00	40.00	150.00
1839	10.00	20.00	40.00	160.00
1839O	45.00	110.00	150.00	350.00

LIBERTY SEATED TYPE

1839–1865

1866–1891

1839 No Drapery from Elbow	22.50	50.00	70.00	350.00
1839 With Drapery	9.00	15.00	25.00	100.00
1840	5.00	10.00	15.00	70.00
1840O	5.00	10.00	15.00	70.00
1841	8.00	15.00	27.00	90.00
1841O	7.00	12.00	20.00	75.00
1842	4.00	8.00	15.00	65.00
1842O	4.00	8.00	15.00	65.00
1843	4.00	8.00	15.00	60.00
1843O	4.00	8.00	15.00	60.00
1844	4.00	8.00	15.00	60.00
1844O	4.00	8.00	15.00	60.00
1845	4.00	8.00	15.00	60.00
1845O	4.00	8.00	15.00	60.00
1845O No Drapery	15.00	35.00	50.00	125.00
1846	4.00	8.00	15.00	60.00
1846 over horizontal 6	35.00	75.00	125.00	300.00
1846O	4.00	8.00	15.00	60.00
1847 over 46	150.00	250.00	500.00	800.00
1847	5.00	9.00	15.00	60.00

	Good	Fine	V. Fine	Unc.
1847O	5.00	9.00	15.00	60.00
1848	5.00	9.00	15.00	60.00
1848O	4.00	8.00	15.00	60.00
1849	5.00	9.00	15.00	60.00
1849O	5.00	8.00	15.00	60.00
1850	25.00	45.00	75.00	160.00
1850O	6.00	10.00	15.00	60.00
1851	25.00	45.00	75.00	160.00
1851O	5.00	10.00	15.00	60.00
1852	25.00	60.00	135.00	250.00
1852O	20.00	30.00	72.50	160.00
1853O No Rays & Arrows (Very rare)	—	—	—	—
1853	7.00	17.50	30.00	300.00
1853O	7.00	20.00	35.00	300.00

	Good	Fine	V. Fine	Unc.	Proof
1854 Arrows at Date	4.00	7.00	14.00	80.00	—
1854O	4.00	7.00	14.00	80.00	—
1855	4.00	9.00	15.00	85.00	850.00
1855O	3.50	7.50	14.00	75.00	—
1855S	32.50	85.00	175.00	500.00	—
1856 No Arrows	3.00	6.00	10.00	45.00	750.00
1856O	3.00	6.00	10.00	45.00	—
1856S	10.00	22.00	75.00	175.00	—
1857	3.00	6.00	10.00	50.00	750.00
1857O	4.00	7.50	14.00	60.00	—
1857S	15.00	35.00	75.00	200.00	—
1858	3.00	6.00	10.00	45.00	375.00
1858O	3.00	6.00	10.00	45.00	—
1858S	6.00	17.50	30.00	125.00	—
1859	3.00	6.00	10.00	45.00	250.00
1859O	3.00	6.00	10.00	45.00	—
1859S	6.50	18.00	30.00	100.00	—
1860	3.00	6.00	10.00	45.00	125.00
1860O	3.00	6.00	10.00	45.00	—
1860S	5.00	12.00	20.00	75.00	—
1861	3.00	6.00	10.00	45.00	125.00
1861O	3.00	6.00	10.00	45.00	—
1861S	4.00	9.00	15.00	65.00	—
1862	3.00	6.00	10.00	45.00	150.00
1862S	4.00	8.00	15.00	55.00	—
1863	4.00	8.00	15.00	55.00	160.00
1863S	4.00	8.00	15.00	55.00	—
1864	4.00	8.00	15.00	55.00	165.00
1864S	4.00	8.00	15.00	55.00	—
1865	4.00	8.00	15.00	55.00	165.00
1865S	4.00	8.00	15.00	55.00	—
1866	4.00	8.00	15.00	50.00	160.00
1866S No Motto	35.00	90.00	180.00	400.00	—
1866S Motto	4.00	8.00	15.00	60.00	—
1867	4.00	8.00	15.00	50.00	150.00
1867S	4.00	8.00	15.00	50.00	—
1868	4.00	8.00	15.00	50.00	140.00
1868S	4.00	8.00	15.00	50.00	—
1869	4.00	8.00	15.00	50.00	140.00
1869S	4.00	8.00	15.00	50.00	—
1870	4.00	8.00	15.00	50.00	125.00

	Good	*Fine*	*V. Fine*	*Unc.*	*Proof*
1870CC	50.00	100.00	200.00	650.00	—
1870S	4.00	8.00	20.00	65.00	—
1871	4.00	8.00	10.00	50.00	125.00
1871CC	40.00	100.00	180.00	500.00	—
1871S	4.00	8.00	12.00	60.00	—
1872	4.00	8.00	12.00	60.00	120.00
1872CC	27.50	70.00	100.00	325.00	—
1872S	4.00	10.00	20.00	65.00	—
1873	4.00	8.00	15.00	65.00	150.00
1873CC	30.00	90.00	125.00	400.00	—
1873 Arrows	15.00	30.00	80.00	225.00	400.00
1873S	18.00	40.00	60.00	250.00	—
1874	13.00	35.00	55.00	200.00	350.00
1874CC	30.00	90.00	150.00	500.00	—
1874S	20.00	50.00	100.00	275.00	—
1875 No Arrows	3.00	7.00	10.00	50.00	110.00
1875 CC	6.50	12.00	25.00	90.00	—
1875S	3.00	7.00	10.00	45.00	—
1876	3.00	7.00	10.00	45.00	110.00
1876CC	5.00	10.00	17.00	55.00	—
1876S	3.00	7.00	10.00	45.00	—
1877	3.00	7.00	10.00	45.00	150.00
1877CC	6.00	12.00	20.00	65.00	—
1877S	3.00	7.00	10.00	45.00	—
1878	3.00	7.00	10.00	45.00	140.00
1878CC	80.00	135.00	220.00	600.00	—
1878S	275.00	550.00	1,150.00	3,000.00	—
1879	40.00	50.00	55.00	90.00	110.00
1880	35.00	45.00	50.00	85.00	110.00
1881	35.00	45.00	50.00	85.00	110.00
1882	35.00	45.00	50.00	85.00	110.00
1883	35.00	45.00	50.00	85.00	125.00
1884	30.00	40.00	45.00	80.00	125.00
1885	30.00	40.00	45.00	80.00	125.00
1886	65.00	75.00	80.00	110.00	140.00
1887	40.00	50.00	55.00	90.00	140.00
1888	30.00	40.00	45.00	80.00	125.00
1889	35.00	45.00	50.00	85.00	140.00
1890	40.00	50.00	55.00	90.00	150.00
1891	4.00	6.00	11.00	60.00	140.00

BARBER OR LIBERTY HEAD TYPE

	Good	Fine	V. Fine	Unc.	Proof
1892	4.00	7.00	20.00	90.00	125.00
1892O	20.00	40.00	65.00	100.00	–
1892S	20.00	45.00	80.00	150.00	–
1893	3.00	6.00	20.00	75.00	140.00
1893O	4.00	7.00	20.00	100.00	–
1893S	20.00	40.00	60.00	125.00	–
1894	3.00	7.00	25.00	75.00	120.00
1894O	4.00	13.00	50.00	100.00	–
1894S	3.00	12.00	45.00	100.00	–
1895	3.00	6.00	20.00	85.00	125.00
1895O	3.00	10.00	40.00	100.00	–
1895S	5.00	9.00	50.00	110.00	–
1896	4.00	8.00	20.00	90.00	125.00
1896O	6.50	17.00	90.00	200.00	–
1896S	20.00	50.00	125.00	325.00	–
1897	2.00	6.00	20.00	80.00	125.00
1897O	20.00	45.00	110.00	275.00	–
1897S	20.00	45.00	115.00	300.00	–
1898	2.00	6.00	20.00	90.00	150.00
1898O	4.00	10.00	40.00	115.00	–
1898S	4.00	9.00	40.00	110.00	–
1899	2.00	5.00	20.00	90.00	125.00
1899O	3.00	8.00	40.00	110.00	–
1899S	4.00	8.00	40.00	110.00	–
1900	1.50	4.00	20.00	85.00	125.00
1900O	1.75	8.00	40.00	100.00	–
1900S	1.75	8.00	35.00	100.00	–
1901	1.75	5.00	20.00	80.00	125.00
1901O	3.00	10.00	125.00	325.00	–
1901S	8.00	40.00	200.00	800.00	–
1902	1.75	4.00	20.00	85.00	125.00
1902O	1.75	7.00	35.00	100.00	–
1902S	1.75	9.00	75.00	200.00	–
1903	1.75	4.00	20.00	90.00	125.00
1903O	1.75	7.50	55.00	175.00	–
1903S	2.50	15.00	100.00	375.00	–
1904	1.75	4.00	20.00	85.00	125.00
1904O	2.00	5.00	35.00	110.00	–
1904S	7.50	20.00	100.00	400.00	–
1905	4.00	7.50	25.00	90.00	125.00
1905O	7.00	14.00	50.00	175.00	–
1905S	2.00	6.50	25.00	100.00	–
1906	1.75	5.00	20.00	90.00	125.00
1906D	1.75	5.00	20.00	90.00	–
1906O	1.75	6.50	20.00	90.00	–
1906S	1.75	8.00	25.00	90.00	–
1907	1.75	5.00	20.00	90.00	125.00
1907D	1.75	5.00	20.00	90.00	–
1907O	1.75	5.00	20.00	90.00	–
1907S	2.00	8.00	30.00	120.00	–
1908	1.75	6.00	20.00	90.00	150.00
1908D	1.75	6.00	20.00	90.00	–
1908O	1.75	6.00	20.00	90.00	–
1908S	1.75	7.50	25.00	90.00	–
1909	1.75	6.00	20.00	90.00	140.00
1909O	1.75	8.50	30.00	90.00	–

	Good	Fine	Ex. Fine	Unc.	Proof
1909S	1.75	6.50	25.00	90.00	–
1910	4.00	10.00	25.00	100.00	200.00
1910S	1.75	6.50	25.00	100.00	–
1911	1.75	5.00	25.00	90.00	200.00
1911D	2.50	6.00	20.00	85.00	–
1911S	1.75	6.00	22.50	85.00	–
1912	1.75	5.00	20.00	90.00	150.00
1912D	1.75	5.00	20.00	90.00	–
1912S	1.75	5.00	20.00	90.00	–
1913	15.00	25.00	55.00	175.00	325.00
1913D	3.00	7.00	25.00	100.00	–
1913S	3.00	8.00	50.00	150.00	–
1914	15.00	40.00	75.00	250.00	550.00
1914S	2.00	8.00	30.00	100.00	–
1915	15.00	35.00	90.00	200.00	500.00
1915D	1.75	5.00	20.00	90.00	–
1915S	1.75	6.50	25.00	100.00	–

LIBERTY WALKING TYPE

	Good	V.G.	Fine	Ex. Fine	Unc.
1916	–	9.00	15.00	35.00	100.00
1916D on Obverse	–	9.00	14.00	30.00	75.00
1916S on Obverse	15.00	25.00	35.00	75.00	200.00
1917	–	–	2.00	9.00	30.00
1917D on Obverse	–	8.00	17.00	50.00	100.00
1917D on Reverse	–	3.00	8.00	45.00	150.00
1917S on Obverse	4.50	10.00	30.00	100.00	425.00
1917S on Reverse	–	–	4.00	20.00	110.00
1918	–	–	4.00	25.00	110.00
1918D	–	–	5.00	40.00	125.00
1918S	–	–	4.00	30.00	110.00
1919	–	–	10.00	50.00	350.00
1919D	–	–	10.00	125.00	500.00
1919S	–	6.00	15.00	150.00	600.00
1920	–	–	3.50	10.00	75.00
1920D	–	–	10.00	70.00	500.00
1920S	–	–	8.00	65.00	400.00
1921	25.00	40.00	50.00	150.00	700.00
1921D	50.00	60.00	80.00	200.00	900.00
1921S	–	12.00	25.00	150.00	1,000.00
1923S	–	–	5.50	75.00	350.00
1927S	–	–	3.00	25.00	125.00
1928S	–	–	3.00	20.00	150.00

	Good	V.G.	Fine	Ex. Fine	Unc.
1929D	–	–	5.00	20.00	90.00
1929S	–	–	3.00	17.00	80.00
1933S	–	–	3.00	20.00	100.00
1934	–	–	–	3.00	10.00
1934D	–	–	–	5.00	35.00
1934S	–	–	–	18.00	60.00
1935	–	–	–	2.50	9.00
1935D	–	–	–	9.00	40.00
1935S	–	–	–	15.00	60.00
1936	–	–	–	2.50	8.00
1936D	–	–	–	3.00	17.00
1936S	–	–	–	6.00	37.00
1937	–	–	–	2.50	10.00
1937D	–	–	–	11.00	55.00
1937S	–	–	–	11.00	50.00
1938	–	–	–	5.00	30.00
1938D	–	–	30.00	50.00	200.00
1939	–	–	–	3.50	10.00
1939D	–	–	–	3.50	14.00
1939S	–	–	–	7.50	25.00
1940	–	–	–	2.00	7.00
1940S	–	–	–	3.00	13.00
1941	–	–	–	2.00	7.00
1941D	–	–	–	2.50	13.00
1941S	–	–	–	4.00	32.00
1942	–	–	–	2.00	6.00
1942D	–	–	–	3.00	14.00
1942S	–	–	–	4.00	16.00
1943	–	–	–	–	6.00
1943D	–	–	–	–	12.00
1943S	–	–	–	–	16.00
1944	–	–	–	–	6.00
1944D	–	–	–	–	7.00
1944S	–	–	–	–	7.00
1945	–	–	–	–	6.00
1945D	–	–	–	–	6.00
1945S	–	–	–	–	7.00
1946	–	–	–	–	7.00
1946D	–	–	–	–	12.00
1946S	–	–	–	–	8.00
1947	–	–	–	–	9.00
1947D	–	–	–	–	8.00

FRANKLIN TYPE

	Unc.
1948	11.00
1948D	6.00
1949	26.00
1949D	20.00
1949S	23.00
1950	17.00
1950D	11.00
1951	4.50
1951D	20.00
1951S	12.00
1952	3.00
1952D	3.00
1952S	11.00
1953	12.00
1953D	2.00
1953S	6.00
1954	2.00
1954D	2.00
1954S	4.00
1955	11.00
1956	4.00
1957	4.00
1957D	3.50
1958	4.00
1958D	1.75
1959	3.00
1959D	2.00
1960	2.50
1960D	1.75
1961	2.00
1961D	2.00
1962	2.00
1962D	1.75
1963	1.50
1963D	1.50
Complete Collection Franklin Halves. 1948–1963D All Mints. Uncirculated. 35 Pieces	252.50

KENNEDY TYPE

	Unc.
1964	1.25
1964D	1.25
1965	1.25
1966	1.00
1967	1.00
1968D	1.00
1969D & S each	1.00

35.
SILVER DOLLARS—
1794–1935

FLOWING HAIR TYPE

	Good	Fine	V. Fine	Unc.
1794	1,000.00	2,500.00	5,000.00	12,500.00
1795	150.00	250.00	400.00	1,000.00

DRAPED BUST TYPE

1795–1798

1798–1804

1795	125.00	250.00	400.00	1,500.00
1796	125.00	250.00	375.00	1,250.00

	Good	Fine	V. Fine	Unc.
1797 9 Stars Left, 7 Right	150.00	300.00	500.00	1,500.00
1797 10 Stars Left, 6 Right	150.00	300.00	450.00	1,500.00
1798 13 Stars	135.00	225.00	350.00	1,100.00
1798 15 Stars	150.00	250.00	400.00	1,250.00
1798 Large eagle	75.00	150.00	200.00	700.00
1799 over 98	75.00	150.00	200.00	700.00
1799 Stars 7 Left, 6 Right	75.00	150.00	200.00	700.00
1799 Stars 8 Left, 5 Right	90.00	175.00	250.00	750.00
1800	75.00	150.00	200.00	600.00
1801	75.00	150.00	200.00	600.00
1802 over 1	75.00	150.00	200.00	600.00
1802	75.00	150.00	200.00	600.00
1803	75.00	150.00	200.00	600.00
1804 Very rare. Record Sales to	77,000.00	–	–	–

GOBRECHT PATTERNS

	Proof
1836 C. Gobrecht F. in field below base. Reverse Eagle in field of stars	3,000.00
1836 Obverse as above Reverse. Eagle flying in plain field	3,250.00

	V. Fine	Proof	–
1836 C. Gobrecht on base	800.00	1,500.00	–
1838	–	3,500.00	–
1839	–	3,500.00	–

LIBERTY SEATED TYPE

1840–1865

1866–1873

	Fine	*Unc.*	*Proof*
1840	35.00	150.00	900.00
1841	30.00	125.00	800.00
1842	30.00	125.00	800.00
1843	30.00	125.00	800.00
1844	70.00	200.00	800.00
1845	70.00	200.00	800.00
1846	25.00	125.00	800.00
1846O	40.00	160.00	–
1847	35.00	150.00	750.00
1848	65.00	200.00	800.00
1849	35.00	150.00	800.00
1850	100.00	300.00	800.00
1850O	40.00	150.00	–
1851	500.00	1,500.00	2,000.00
1852	–	2,500.00	–
1853	60.00	275.00	1,400.00
1854	100.00	350.00	1,000.00
1855	125.00	375.00	1,000.00
1856	60.00	275.00	800.00
1857	60.00	250.00	650.00
1858	–	–	2,000.00
1859	35.00	150.00	300.00
1859O	30.00	125.00	–
1859S	70.00	300.00	–
1860	35.00	125.00	250.00
1860O	30.00	90.00	–
1861	50.00	150.00	300.00
1862	50.00	250.00	400.00
1863	50.00	200.00	400.00
1864	50.00	175.00	400.00
1865	50.00	175.00	400.00
1866	50.00	175.00	350.00
1867	50.00	175.00	350.00
1868	40.00	125.00	350.00
1869	30.00	125.00	350.00

	Fine	Unc.	Proof
1870	30.00	100.00	300.00
1870CC	100.00	500.00	–
1870S	–	–	–
1871	25.00	100.00	300.00
1871CC	600.00	2,000.00	–
1872	25.00	100.00	300.00
1872CC	300.00	1,200.00	–
1872S	75.00	350.00	–
1873	30.00	125.00	300.00
1873CC	800.00	2,500.00	–

MORGAN OR LIBERTY HEAD TYPE

	Ex. Fine	Unc.	Proof
1878 8 Tail Feathers	6.00	15.00	300.00
1878 7 Tail Feathers over 8 Tail Feathers	12.00	17.00	–
1878 7 Tail Feathers	3.00	5.00	350.00
1878CC	7.00	15.00	–
1878S	2.50	4.00	–
1879	2.00	4.00	200.00
1879CC	40.00	200.00	–
1879O	3.00	7.00	–
1879S	2.50	4.00	–
1880	2.50	4.50	200.00
1880CC	30.00	55.00	–
1880O	3.00	6.00	–
1880S	2.50	3.50	–
1881	2.50	5.00	200.00
1881CC	55.00	75.00	–
1881O	2.50	4.00	–
1881S	2.50	4.00	–
1882	2.50	4.00	200.00
1882CC	15.00	30.00	–
1882O	2.50	4.00	–
1882S	2.50	4.00	–
1883	2.50	4.00	200.00
1883CC	20.00	30.00	–
1883O	2.50	4.00	–
1883S	5.00	30.00	–

	Ex. Fine	Unc.	Proof
1884	2.50	4.00	200.00
1884CC	25.00	35.00	—
1884O	2.50	4.00	—
1884S	5.00	50.00	—
1885	2.50	4.00	200.00
1885CC	40.00	65.00	—
1885O	2.50	4.00	—
1885S	5.00	15.00	—
1886	2.50	4.00	200.00
1886O	4.00	17.00	—
1886S	15.00	35.00	—
1887	2.50	4.00	200.00
1887O	2.50	5.00	—
1887S	7.00	15.00	—
1888	2.50	4.00	200.00
1888O	3.00	5.00	—
1888S	25.00	40.00	—
1889	2.50	4.00	200.00
1889CC	175.00	850.00	—
1889O	4.00	14.00	—
1889S	20.00	35.00	—
1890	2.50	4.00	225.00
1890CC	10.00	30.00	—
1890O	3.00	8.00	—
1890S	3.00	9.00	—
1891	4.00	12.00	250.00
1891CC	10.00	30.00	—
1891O	4.00	13.00	—
1891S	5.00	15.00	—
1892	5.00	20.00	200.00
1892CC	30.00	60.00	—
1892O	5.00	25.00	—
1892S	30.00	1,000.00	—
1893	15.00	50.00	250.00
1893CC	50.00	200.00	—
1893O	35.00	200.00	—
1893S	500.00	4,500.00	—
1894	75.00	200.00	650.00
1894O	10.00	60.00	—
1894S	15.00	50.00	—
1895	—	—	4,000.00
1895O	30.00	225.00	—
1895S	75.00	500.00	—
1896	2.50	4.00	220.00
1896O	6.50	45.00	—
1896S	30.00	200.00	—
1897	3.00	7.00	200.00
1897O	6.50	35.00	—
1897S	3.50	13.00	—
1898	3.00	5.00	200.00
1898O	2.50	4.00	—
1898S	8.00	30.00	—
1899	15.00	25.00	250.00
1899O	2.50	4.00	—
1899S	10.00	40.00	—
1900	2.50	4.00	200.00
1900O	2.50	4.00	—

	Ex. Fine	Unc.	Proof
1900S	5.50	25.00	–
1901	10.00	80.00	200.00
1901O	2.50	4.00	–
1901S	10.00	40.00	–
1902	3.50	9.00	220.00
1902O	2.50	4.00	–
1902S	35.00	90.00	–
1903	4.00	8.00	220.00
1903O	30.00	40.00	–
1903S	35.00	325.00	–
1904	5.00	20.00	250.00
1904O	2.50	4.00	–
1904S	20.00	175.00	–
1921	2.50	4.00	–
1921D	2.50	4.00	–
1921S	2.50	4.00	–

(Note: All Liberty Head Dollars good or better have a minimum valve of from $1.75 to $2.00 each.)

PEACE TYPE

	Ex. Fine	Unc.	Proof
1921	15.00	30.00	–
1922	2.50	4.00	–
1922D	2.50	5.00	–
1922S	2.50	6.00	–
1923	2.50	4.00	–
1923D	4.00	12.00	–
1923S	2.50	6.00	–
1924	2.50	5.00	–
1924S	10.00	38.00	–
1925	2.50	5.00	–
1925S	6.00	20.00	–
1926	6.00	10.00	–
1926D	5.00	11.00	–
1926S	3.00	8.00	–
1927	20.00	30.00	–
1927D	12.00	35.00	–
1927S	13.00	45.00	–

	Ex. Fine	Unc.	Proof
1928	60.00	100.00	–
1928S	7.00	25.00	–
1934	10.00	22.50	–
1934D	10.00	30.00	–
1934S	35.00	230.00	–
1935	8.00	17.00	–
1935S	10.00	40.00	–
Complete Collection Peace Dollars. 1921–1935S All Mints. Uncirculated. 24 Pieces	–	708.50	–

(Note: All Peace Dollars good or better have a minimum value of from $1.75 to $2.00 each.)

36.

TRADE DOLLARS—1873–1885

	V.G.	*Fine*	*Ex. Fine*	*Unc.*	*Proof*
1873	20.00	30.00	50.00	150.00	400.00
1873CC	25.00	50.00	100.00	250.00	—
1873S	20.00	30.00	60.00	150.00	—
1874	15.00	25.00	40.00	90.00	300.00
1874CC	25.00	45.00	80.00	175.00	—
1874S	20.00	30.00	50.00	160.00	—
1875	25.00	40.00	75.00	150.00	300.00
1875CC	25.00	40.00	75.00	150.00	—
1875S	15.00	25.00	35.00	85.00	—
1876	20.00	25.00	45.00	100.00	300.00
1876CC	25.00	40.00	70.00	150.00	—
1876S	15.00	25.00	35.00	85.00	—
1877	15.00	25.00	35.00	85.00	425.00
1877CC	30.00	50.00	110.00	225.00	—
1877S	15.00	20.00	35.00	85.00	—
1878	—	—	—	—	450.00
1878CC	75.00	150.00	250.00	500.00	—
1878S	15.00	20.00	35.00	85.00	—
1879	—	—	—	—	325.00
1880	—	—	—	—	325.00
1881	—	—	—	—	375.00
1882	—	—	—	—	350.00

	V.G.	*Fine*	*Ex. Fine*	*Unc.*	*Proof*
1883	–	–	–	–	375.00
1884	–	–	–	–	8,750.00
1885	–	–	–	–	9,000.00

37.

SILVER COMMEMORATIVE COINS

(Half Dollars unless otherwise specified)

Year	*Unc.*
1892 Columbian Exposition	8.00
1893 Columbian Exposition	6.00
1893 Isabella Quarter	90.00
1900 Lafayette Dollar	175.00
1915 S Panama-Pacific Exposition	85.00
1918 Illinois Centennial	27.00
1920 Maine Centennial	28.50
1920 Pilgrim Tercentenary	15.00
1921 Pilgrim Tercentenary (1921) on obverse	22.50
1921 Missouri Centennial (with star)	170.00
1921 Missouri Centennial (no star)	145.00
1921 Alabama Centennial (with 2 x 2)	50.00
1921 Alabama Centennial (no 2 x 2)	47.50
1922 Grant Memorial (with star)	135.00
1922 Grant Memorial (no star)	26.50
1923 S Monroe Doctrine Centennial	16.50
1924 Huguenot-Walloon Tercentenary	29.00
1925 Lexington-Concord Sesquicentennial	16.50
1925 Stone Mountain Memorial	11.00
1925 S California Diamond Jubilee	25.00
1925 Fort Vancouver Centennial	92.50
1926 Sesquicentennial of American Independence	17.50
1926 Oregon Trail Memorial	15.50
1926 S Oregon Trail Memorial	15.50
1928 Oregon Trail Memorial	15.50
1933 D Oregon Trail Memorial	37.50
1934 D Oregon Trail Memorial	16.50
1936 Oregon Trail Memorial	15.50
1936 S Oregon Trail Memorial	18.50
1937 D Oregon Trail Memorial	16.00
1938 P-D-S Oregon Trail Memorial (set of three)	46.00
1939 P-D-S Oregon Trail Memorial (set of three)	130.00
1927 Vermont Sesquicentennial	38.50
1928 Hawaiian Sesquicentennial	485.00
1934 Maryland Tercentenary	33.50
1934 Texas Centennial	18.50
1935 P-D-S Texas Centennial (set of three)	48.50
1936 P-D-S Texas Centennial (set of three)	48.50
1937 P-D-S Texas Centennial (set of three)	48.50
1938 P-D-S Texas Centennial (set of three)	127.50
1934 Daniel Boone Bicentennial	18.50
1935 P-D-S Daniel Boone Bicentennial (set of three)	42.50

Year	Unc.
1935 P-D-S Daniel Boone Bicentennial (set of three)*	325.00
1936 P-D-S Daniel Boone Bicentennial (set of three)	45.00
1937 P-D-S Daniel Boone Bicentennial (set of three)	195.00
1938 P-D-S Daniel Boone Bicentennial (set of three)	325.00
1935 Connecticut Tercentenary	52.00
1935 P-D-S Arkansas Centennial (set of three)	39.50
1936 P-D-S Arkansas Centennial (set of three)	39.50
1937 P-D-S Arkansas Centennial (set of three)	39.50
1938 P-D-S Arkansas Centennial (set of three)	67.50
1939 P-D-S Arkansas Centennial (set of three)	330.00
1935 Hudson, N.Y. Sesquicentennial	265.00
1935 S California-Pacific Exposition	16.50
1936 D California-Pacific Exposition	18.00
1935 Old Spanish Trail	235.00
1936 P-D-S Rhode Island Tercentenary (set of three)	58.50
1936 Cleveland, Great Lakes Exposition	18.75
1936 Wisconsin Territorial Centennial	34.50
1936 P-D-S Cincinnati Musical Center (set of three)	385.00
1936 Long Island Tercentenary	17.50
1936 York County, Maine Tercentenary	25.00
1936 Bridgeport, Conn. Centennial	24.50
1936 Lynchburg, Va. Sesquicentennial	36.50
1936 Elgin, Illinois Centennial	35.00
1936 Albany, N.Y. Charter	50.00
1936 S San Francisco-Oakland Bay Bridge	22.50
1936 P-D-S Columbia, S.C. Sesquicentennial (set of three)	108.00
1936 Arkansas Centennial-Robinson	23.00
1936 Delaware Tercentenary	46.50
1936 Battle of Gettysburg (1863–1938)	42.50
1936 Norfolk, Va. Bicentennial	57.50
1937 Roanoke Island, N.C. (1587–1937)	27.50
1937 Battle of Antietam (1862–1937)	79.50
1938 New Rochelle, N.Y. (1688–1938)	65.00
1946 Iowa Centennial	24.50
1946 P-D-S Booker T. Washington Memorial (set of three)	12.00
1947 P-D-S Booker T. Washington Memorial (set of three)	15.50
1948 P-D-S Booker T. Washington Memorial (set of three)	22.50
1949 P-D-S Booker T. Washington Memorial (set of three)	39.50
1950 P-D-S Booker T. Washington Memorial (set of three)	33.00
1951 P-D-S Booker T. Washington Memorial (set of three)	31.50
1951 P-D-S Washington-Carver (set of three)	12.50
1952 P-D-S Washington-Carver (set of three)	19.50
1953 P-D-S Washington-Carver (set of three)	22.50
1954 P-D-S Washington-Carver (set of three)	12.00

*Small "1934" added on Reverse.

38.

GOLD COMMEMORATIVE COINS

(Dollar unless otherwise specified)

Year	*Unc.*
1903 Louisiana Purchase (Jefferson)	80.00
1903 Louisiana Purchase (McKinley)	75.00
1904 Lewis and Clark Exposition	300.00
1905 Lewis and Clark Exposition	310.00
1915 S Panama-Pacific Exposition	67.50
1915 S Panama-Pacific Exposition ($2.50)	300.00
1915 S Panama-Pacific Exposition ($50 round)	5,000.00
1915 S Panama-Pacific Exposition ($50 octagonal)	3,750.00
1916 McKinley Memorial	75.00
1917 McKinley Memorial	77.50
1922 Grant Memorial (with star)	230.00
1922 Grant Memorial (no star)	235.00
1926 Philadelphia Sesquicentennial (2.50)	65.00
Set–Commemorative Gold without the two $50 pieces. 11 coins	1,815.00

39.

PROOF SETS

EACH SET CONTAINS A HALF, QUARTER, DIME, NICKEL AND CENT, SPECIALLY STRUCK AT THE MINT WITH MIRROR-LIKE FINISH

Date and Number of Sets Coined	*Proof*
1936 (3,837)	750.00
1937 (5,542)	275.00
1938 (8,045)	150.00
1939 (8,795)	125.00
1940 (11,246)	100.00
1941 (15,287)	90.00
1942 (21,120) 6 pieces	110.00
1950 (51,386)	100.00
1951 (57,500)	65.00
1952 (81,980)	35.00
1953 (128,800)	25.00
1954 (233,300)	16.00
1955 (378,200)	23.00
1956 (669,384)	11.00
1957 (1,247,952)	6.00
1958 (875,652)	14.50
1959 (1,149,291)	8.00
1960 (1,691,602)	5.75
1960 with sm. dt. ct.	22.00
1961 (3,028,244)	4.00
1962 (3,218,039)	4.00
1963	4.00
1964	6.00
1968S Proof Sets	7.25
1969S Proof Sets	6.25
1970S Proof Sets	7.00

40.

ROLLS OF BRILLANT UNCIRCULATED COINS

50 CENTS TO THE ROLL

40 NICKELS TO THE ROLL

	Cents	*Nickels*
1935-P	40.00	–
1935-D	40.00	–
1935-S	80.00	–
1936-P	27.50	–
1936-D	30.00	–
1936-S	40.00	–
1937-P	27.50	–
1937-D	25.00	–
1937-S	28.00	–
1938-P	30.00	32.00
1938-D	45.00	160.00
1938-S	65.00	180.00
1939-P	20.00	32.00
1939-D	95.00	1,300.00
1939-S	24.00	340.00
1940-P	13.00	20.00
1940-D	21.00	36.00
1940-S	12.00	58.00
1941-P	15.00	20.00
1941-D	37.00	28.50
1941-S	41.00	33.00
1942-P	8.00	T1 40.00
		T2 175.50
1942-D	9.00	255.00
1942-S	95.00	100.00
1943-P	8.00	36.50
1943-D	16.00	105.00
1943-S	27.00	36.00
1944-P	5.00	50.00
1944-D	4.25	72.00
1944-S	7.50	73.00
1945-P	9.00	86.00
1945-D	8.00	45.00
1945-S	9.00	35.00
1946-P	5.00	7.00
1946-D	5.00	21.00
1946-S	5.00	28.00
1947-P	14.00	10.00
1947-D	6.00	22.50

	Cents	*Nickels*
1947-S	25.00	22.00
1948-P	11.00	9.00
1948-D	6.00	61.00
1948-S	25.00	28.00
1949-P	14.00	16.00
1949-D	10.00	31.00
1949-S	27.00	61.00
1950-P	14.00	57.00
1950-D	6.00	365.00
1950-S	13.00	—
1951-P	16.50	23.00
1951-D	4.50	37.50
1951-S	24.00	90.00
1952-P	14.00	12.50
1952-D	3.00	52.00
1952-S	14.50	20.00
1953-P	6.00	5.50
1953-D	3.00	11.00
1953-S	7.00	12.00
1954-P	13.00	5.25
1954-D	3.00	5.00
1954-S	6.00	8.00
1955-P	4.00	41.00
1955-D	3.00	6.00
1955-S	14.00	—
1956-P	2.50	5.00
1956-D	1.50	4.00
1957-P	2.00	5.00
1957-D	1.25	3.50
1958-P	1.85	12.00
1958-D	1.25	3.00
1959-P	1.25	5.25
1959-D	1.00	3.00
1960-P-D	1.00	3.00
1960-P-D-S	1.00	—
1961-P-D	1.00	3.00
1962-P-D	1.00	3.00
1963-P-D	1.00	3.00
1964-P-D	1.00	3.00
1965-P-D	1.00	3.00
1966-P-D	1.00	3.00
1967-P-D	1.00	3.00
1968-P	1.25	3.00
1968-D-S	1.00	3.00
1969-P-D-S	1.00	3.00
1970-P-D-S	1.00	3.00

41.

GOLD DOLLARS– 1849–1889

LIBERTY HEAD TYPE

	V. Fine	*Unc.*	*Proof*
1849	45.00	80.00	–
1849C	175.00	500.00	–
1849D	200.00	400.00	–
1849O	50.00	80.00	–
1850	50.00	70.00	–
1850C	250.00	575.00	–
1850D	200.00	425.00	–
1850O	70.00	160.00	–
1851	45.00	70.00	–
1851C	150.00	250.00	–
1851D	175.00	400.00	–
1851O	55.00	70.00	–
1852	50.00	70.00	–
1852C	200.00	400.00	–
1852D	200.00	400.00	–
1852O	50.00	75.00	–
1853	50.00	60.00	–
1853C	145.00	350.00	–
1853D	200.00	425.00	–
1853O	50.00	75.00	–
1854 Small Planchet	45.00	70.00	–
1854D	350.00	800.00	–
1854S	125.00	300.00	–

INDIAN HEADDRESS TYPE

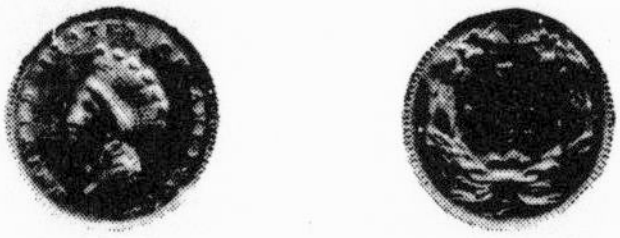

	V. Fine	*Unc.*	*Proof*
1854 Large Planchet	150.00	400.00	–
1855	150.00	400.00	–
1855C	250.00	450.00	–
1855D	1,250.00	3,000.00	–
1855O	150.00	400.00	–
1856S	175.00	450.00	–

LARGER INDIAN HEADDRESS TYPE

1856	50.00	65.00	1,000.00
1856D	1,500.00	3,000.00	–
1857	40.00	65.00	1,000.00
1857C	175.00	400.00	–
1857D	375.00	800.00	–
1857S	100.00	200.00	–
1858	50.00	80.00	800.00
1858D	600.00	1,200.00	–
1858S	120.00	225.00	–
1859	40.00	65.00	600.00
1859C	225.00	475.00	–
1859D	275.00	500.00	–
1859S	125.00	200.00	–
1860	50.00	80.00	500.00
1860D	2,500.00	4,000.00	–
1860S	125.00	225.00	–
1861	40.00	65.00	500.00
1861D	3,750.00	7,500.00	–
1862	40.00	65.00	500.00
1863	250.00	475.00	800.00
1864	175.00	400.00	900.00
1865	225.00	400.00	600.00
1866	150.00	250.00	500.00
1867	160.00	275.00	500.00
1868	120.00	185.00	500.00
1869	145.00	250.00	500.00
1870	125.00	250.00	500.00
1870S	400.00	1,000.00	–
1871	125.00	225.00	500.00

	V. Fine	*Unc.*	*Proof*
1872	125.00	225.00	500.00
1873	50.00	90.00	500.00
1874	50.00	90.00	500.00
1875	1,000.00	1,750.00	3,500.00
1876	125.00	225.00	500.00
1877	125.00	225.00	500.00
1878	125.00	225.00	500.00
1879	125.00	225.00	500.00
1880	125.00	225.00	500.00
1881	80.00	140.00	375.00
1882	80.00	140.00	375.00
1883	80.00	140.00	375.00
1884	90.00	140.00	250.00
1885	80.00	125.00	250.00
1886	80.00	125.00	250.00
1887	80.00	125.00	250.00
1888	80.00	125.00	250.00
1889	80.00	100.00	250.00

42. QUARTER EAGLES– 1796–1929

($2.50 GOLD PIECES)

LIBERTY CAP TYPE

1796

1796–1807

	V. Fine	*Unc.*	*Proof*
1796 No Stars	5,500.00	7,500.00	–
1796 Stars	5,500.00	8,000.00	–
1797	2,000.00	3,000.00	–
1798	2,000.00	4,500.00	–
1802 over 1	900.00	2,100.00	–
1804	900.00	1,800.00	–
1805	900.00	1,800.00	–
1806 over 4	1,500.00	2,500.00	–
1806 over 5	1,500.00	3,000.00	–
1807	700.00	1,400.00	–

TURBAN HEAD TYPE

1808

1821–1834

1808	4,000.00	6,700.00	–
1821	800.00	2,500.00	–
1824 over 21	850.00	2,200.00	–
1825	1,000.00	3,000.00	–
1826 over 25	2,000.00	3,000.00	–
1827	800.00	2,000.00	–

	V. Fine	Unc.	Proof
1829	700.00	1,100.00	–
1830	500.00	900.00	–
1831	500.00	900.00	–
1832	500.00	900.00	–
1833	500.00	900.00	–
1834 With Motto	1,800.00	3,000.00	–

LIBERTY HEAD TYPE

1834 No Motto	90.00	150.00	–
1835	75.00	150.00	–
1836	75.00	150.00	–
1837	100.00	175.00	–
1838	100.00	175.00	–
1838C	225.00	400.00	–
1839	90.00	175.00	–
1839C	200.00	375.00	–
1839D	200.00	400.00	–
1839O	130.00	200.00	–

CORONET TYPE

1840	70.00	125.00	–
1840C	135.00	300.00	–
1840D	200.00	600.00	–
1840O	70.00	130.00	–
1841 Ex. Rare	–	–	–
1841C	200.00	400.00	–
1841D	300.00	425.00	–
1842	225.00	375.00	–
1842C	185.00	350.00	–
1842D	200.00	400.00	–
1842O	70.00	110.00	–
1843	60.00	80.00	–
1843C	100.00	175.00	–
1843D	125.00	200.00	–
1843O	50.00	75.00	–
1844	140.00	200.00	–
1844C	130.00	200.00	–
1844D	120.00	200.00	–
1845	55.00	80.00	–

	V. Fine	Unc.	Proof
1845D	125.00	225.00	—
1845O	200.00	300.00	—
1846	50.00	85.00	—
1846C	200.00	350.00	—
1846D	125.00	200.00	—
1846O	50.00	90.00	—
1847	50.00	90.00	—
1847C	125.00	250.00	—
1847D	150.00	300.00	—
1847O	50.00	75.00	—
1848	500.00	1,000.00	—
1848 CAL above Eagle	3,000.00	6,000.00	—
1848C	120.00	300.00	—
1848D	150.00	350.00	—
1849	50.00	100.00	—
1849C	125.00	250.00	—
1849D	175.00	300.00	—
1850	50.00	75.00	—
1850C	125.00	250.00	—
1850D	125.00	250.00	—
1850O	50.00	75.00	—
1851	40.00	50.00	—
1851C	150.00	350.00	—
1851D	150.00	375.00	—
1851O	50.00	75.00	—
1852	40.00	50.00	—
1852C	150.00	275.00	—
1852D	300.00	450.00	—
1852O	40.00	50.00	—
1853	40.00	50.00	—
1853D	400.00	800.00	—
1854	40.00	50.00	—
1854C	150.00	350.00	—
1854D	1,200.00	2,500.00	—
1854O	40.00	50.00	—
1854S	4,000.00	7,500.00	—
1855	40.00	50.00	4,000.00
1855C	350.00	600.00	—
1855D	700.00	2,000.00	—
1856	40.00	50.00	3,500.00
1856C	150.00	300.00	—
1856D	1,500.00	4,000.00	—
1856O	40.00	60.00	—
1856S	40.00	90.00	—
1857	40.00	50.00	2,500.00
1857D	400.00	700.00	—
1857O	40.00	60.00	—
1857S	40.00	65.00	—
1858	40.00	50.00	1,500.00
1858C	150.00	350.00	—
1859	40.00	50.00	1,000.00
1859D	350.00	700.00	—
1859S	60.00	125.00	—
1860	40.00	50.00	1,000.00
1860C	150.00	300.00	—
1860S	70.00	150.00	—
1861	40.00	50.00	1,000.00

	V. Fine	Unc.	Proof
1861S	50.00	125.00	–
1862	40.00	50.00	1,200.00
1862S	100.00	200.00	–
1863	–	–	4,000.00
1863S	90.00	175.00	–
1864	300.00	400.00	1,500.00
1865	350.00	500.00	1,400.00
1865S	40.00	50.00	–
1866	200.00	300.00	900.00
1866S	40.00	50.00	–
1867	150.00	300.00	850.00
1867S	50.00	80.00	–
1868	125.00	250.00	900.00
1868S	50.00	100.00	–
1869	100.00	200.00	900.00
1869S	50.00	80.00	–
1870	100.00	175.00	800.00
1870S	50.00	100.00	–
1871	100.00	200.00	750.00
1871S	75.00	100.00	–
1872	150.00	250.00	750.00
1872S	55.00	85.00	–
1873	40.00	50.00	850.00
1873S	50.00	70.00	–
1874	100.00	200.00	1,000.00
1875	500.00	1,300.00	3,000.00
1875S	75.00	150.00	–
1876	120.00	220.00	850.00
1876S	75.00	150.00	–
1877	200.00	400.00	1,200.00
1877S	40.00	50.00	–
1878	40.00	50.00	1,000.00
1878S	40.00	50.00	–
1879	40.00	50.00	600.00
1879S	40.00	50.00	–
1880	150.00	250.00	830.00
1881	375.00	650.00	1,000.00
1882	150.00	250.00	850.00
1883	200.00	300.00	900.00
1884	200.00	300.00	900.00
1885	350.00	550.00	1,100.00
1886	125.00	225.00	600.00
1887	100.00	150.00	600.00
1888	45.00	50.00	500.00
1889	70.00	125.00	500.00
1890	80.00	125.00	500.00
1891	65.00	90.00	450.00
1892	125.00	240.00	500.00
1893	45.00	50.00	500.00
1894	100.00	150.00	600.00
1895	80.00	125.00	500.00
1896	45.00	50.00	450.00
1897	40.00	50.00	400.00
1898	40.00	50.00	400.00
1899	40.00	50.00	400.00
1900	40.00	50.00	350.00
1901	40.00	50.00	350.00

	V. Fine	Unc.	Proof
1902	40.00	50.00	350.00
1903	40.00	50.00	350.00
1904	40.00	50.00	350.00
1905	40.00	50.00	350.00
1906	40.00	50.00	350.00
1907	40.00	50.00	350.00

INDIAN HEAD TYPE

	V. Fine	Unc.	Proof
1908	33.00	37.00	500.00
1909	33.00	37.00	500.00
1910	33.00	37.00	500.00
1911	33.00	37.00	500.00
1911D	325.00	475.00	–
1912	33.00	37.00	500.00
1913	33.00	37.00	500.00
1914	33.00	37.00	550.00
1914D	33.00	37.00	–
1915	33.00	37.00	550.00
1925D	33.00	37.00	–
1926	33.00	37.00	–
1927	33.00	37.00	–
1928	33.00	37.00	–
1929	33.00	37.00	–
Complete Collection Indian Head Quarter Eagles. 15 Pieces	785.00	–	–

43.
THREE-DOLLAR GOLD PIECES–
1854–1889

	V. Fine	Unc.	Proof
1854	225.00	350.00	–
1854D	1,700.00	2,500.00	–
1854O	250.00	350.00	–
1855	175.00	275.00	–
1855S	250.00	450.00	–
1856	175.00	275.00	–
1856S	225.00	350.00	–
1857	175.00	275.00	–
1857S	250.00	350.00	–
1858	375.00	800.00	2,000.00
1859	175.00	275.00	1,200.00
1860	250.00	375.00	1,200.00
1860S	250.00	375.00	–
1861	250.00	375.00	1,500.00
1862	250.00	375.00	1,500.00
1863	250.00	400.00	1,700.00
1864	325.00	600.00	1,800.00
1865	400.00	800.00	1,800.00
1866	250.00	350.00	1,600.00
1867	250.00	400.00	1,600.00
1868	250.00	350.00	1,600.00
1869	260.00	400.00	1,600.00
1870	260.00	400.00	1,600.00
1870S *Very rare*	–	–	–
1871	300.00	500.00	1,800.00
1872	300.00	450.00	1,800.00
1873	–	–	3,000.00
1874	175.00	275.00	2,000.00
1875	–	–	20,000.00
1876	–	–	7,250.00
1877	600.00	1,200.00	3,000.00

	V. Fine	Unc.	Proof
1878	175.00	275.00	2,000.00
1879	250.00	375.00	1,300.00
1880	300.00	500.00	1,400.00
1881	500.00	900.00	2,000.00
1882	300.00	450.00	1,200.00
1883	375.00	500.00	1,200.00
1884	300.00	500.00	1,200.00
1885	350.00	700.00	2,000.00
1886	325.00	600.00	1,200.00
1887	250.00	350.00	1,000.00
1888	250.00	350.00	900.00
1889	300.00	450.00	1,000.00

44.
"STELLA" OR FOUR-DOLLAR GOLD PIECES

	Proof
1879 Flowing hair	5,750.00
1879 Coiled hair	12,500.00
1880 Flowing hair	11,000.00
1880 Coiled hair	13,500.00

45.
HALF EAGLES–
1795–1929

($5 GOLD PIECES)

BUST TYPE

1795–1798

1795–1807

	V. Fine	Unc.	
1795 Small eagle	1,000.00	1,900.00	–
1795 Large eagle	2,000.00	4,000.00	–
1796 over 95	1,000.00	2,000.00	–
1797 15 Stars	1,500.00	3,000.00	–
1797 16 Stars	1,500.00	3,000.00	–
1798 Small eagle (Very rare)	–	–	–
1797 over 95	1,500.00	3,000.00	–
1798 Large eagle, 13 star reverse	500.00	1,000.00	–
1798 Large eagle, 14 star reverse	500.00	1,000.00	–
1799	350.00	700.00	–
1800	350.00	600.00	–
1802 over 1	350.00	600.00	–
1803 over 2	350.00	600.00	–
1804	350.00	600.00	–
1805	350.00	600.00	–
1806	350.00	600.00	–
1807	350.00	600.00	–

LIBERTY CAP TYPE

1807–1812

1813–1834

	V. Fine	*Unc.*	
1807	350.00	600.00	–
1808 over 7	350.00	500.00	–
1808	350.00	500.00	–
1809 over 8	350.00	500.00	–
1809	350.00	500.00	–
1810	350.00	500.00	–
1811	350.00	500.00	–
1812	350.00	500.00	–
1813	350.00	500.00	–
1814	350.00	500.00	–
1815	–	5,000.00	–
1818	350.00	600.00	–
1819	4,000.00	7,500.00	–
1820	500.00	1,000.00	–
1821	1,500.00	3,500.00	–
1822 (Very rare)	–	–	–
1823	750.00	1,500.00	–
1824	–	7,000.00	–
1825 over 21	1,100.00	2,500.00	–
1825 over 24	3,000.00	4,000.00	–
1826	2,000.00	3,500.00	–
1827	2,750.00	7,000.00	–
1828 over 27	–	5,250.00	–
1828	2,900.00	6,000.00	–
1829	–	21,500.00	–
1830	1,000.00	2,000.00	–
1831	750.00	1,500.00	–
1832	2,250.00	4,000.00	–
1833	1,000.00	2,000.00	–
1834	1,000.00	2,000.00	–

TURBAN HEAD TYPE

	V. Fine	Unc.	—
1834	75.00	150.00	—
1835	75.00	150.00	—
1836	75.00	150.00	—
1837	75.00	150.00	—
1838	75.00	150.00	—
1838C	300.00	600.00	—
1838D	250.00	550.00	—

CORONET TYPE

1839–1865

1865–1908

1839	55.00	150.00	—
1839C	200.00	400.00	—
1839D	200.00	450.00	—
1840	50.00	125.00	—
1840C	150.00	325.00	—
1840D	150.00	300.00	—
1840O	100.00	250.00	—
1841	90.00	250.00	—
1841C	150.00	300.00	—
1841D	150.00	300.00	—
1842	75.00	175.00	—
1842C	125.00	225.00	—
1842D	125.00	225.00	—
1842O	110.00	200.00	—
1843	50.00	85.00	—
1843C	125.00	250.00	—
1843D	125.00	250.00	—
1843O	70.00	150.00	—
1844	50.00	125.00	—
1844C	125.00	225.00	—
1844D	125.00	225.00	—
1844O	60.00	200.00	—
1845	50.00	90.00	—
1845D	100.00	250.00	—
1845O	100.00	200.00	—
1846	50.00	85.00	—
1846C	125.00	300.00	—
1846D	125.00	250.00	—
1846O	80.00	150.00	—
1847	50.00	75.00	—
1847C	100.00	225.00	—
1847D	150.00	250.00	—
1847O	100.00	225.00	—
1848	50.00	80.00	—

	V. Fine	Unc.	Proof
1848C	125.00	200.00	—
1848D	175.00	250.00	—

	V. Fine	Unc.	Proof
1849	50.00	65.00	—
1849C	100.00	200.00	—
1849D	125.00	250.00	—
1850	50.00	90.00	—
1850C	110.00	225.00	—
1850D	125.00	250.00	—
1851	50.00	80.00	—
1851C	150.00	275.00	—
1851D	125.00	250.00	—
1851O	60.00	125.00	—
1852	50.00	80.00	—
1852C	125.00	275.00	—
1852D	125.00	250.00	—
1853	50.00	60.00	—
1853C	100.00	225.00	—
1853D	100.00	250.00	—
1854	45.00	70.00	—
1854C	125.00	225.00	—
1854D	110.00	225.00	—
1854O	75.00	150.00	—
1854S		16,500.00	*Ex. F.*
1855	45.00	70.00	3,000.00
1855C	110.00	200.00	—
1855D	120.00	300.00	—
1855O	125.00	250.00	—
1855S	80.00	150.00	—
1856	45.00	80.00	3,000.00
1856C	100.00	200.00	—
1856D	150.00	275.00	—
1856O	175.00	450.00	—
1856S	50.00	100.00	—
1857	45.00	70.00	2,500.00
1857C	125.00	225.00	—
1857D	125.00	250.00	—
1857O	100.00	200.00	—
1857S	60.00	100.00	—
1858	150.00	250.00	1,500.00
1858C	125.00	200.00	—
1858D	125.00	250.00	—
1858S	100.00	150.00	—
1859	125.00	250.00	1,200.00
1859C	125.00	225.00	—
1859D	175.00	350.00	—
1859S	100.00	150.00	—
1860	75.00	150.00	750.00
1860C	125.00	250.00	—
1860D	160.00	350.00	—
1860S	70.00	125.00	—
1861	45.00	75.00	750.00
1861C	400.00	800.00	—
1861D	1,500.00	2,500.00	—
1861S	75.00	150.00	—
1862	250.00	400.00	750.00
1862S	125.00	300.00	—
1863	275.00	500.00	850.00
1863S	100.00	200.00	—
1864	250.00	500.00	1,200.00

	V. Fine	Unc.	Proof
1864S	300.00	750.00	–
1865	300.00	550.00	850.00
1865S	100.00	200.00	–
1866	150.00	300.00	–
1866 Motto on Reverse	200.00	350.00	700.00
1866S	200.00	350.00	–
1867	175.00	300.00	600.00
1867S	75.00	150.00	–
1868	175.00	275.00	700.00
1868S	75.00	200.00	–
1869	300.00	650.00	1,000.00
1869S	75.00	200.00	–
1870	175.00	300.00	900.00
1870CC	600.00	1,000.00	–
1870S	100.00	200.00	–
1871	225.00	450.00	900.00
1871CC	200.00	450.00	–
1871S	100.00	200.00	–
1872	375.00	600.00	1,000.00
1872CC	200.00	500.00	–
1872S	70.00	175.00	–
1873	60.00	100.00	800.00
1873CC	250.00	500.00	–
1873S	80.00	150.00	–
1874	200.00	400.00	900.00
1874CC	200.00	375.00	–
1874S	60.00	125.00	–
1875	1,500.00	3,000.00	4,000.00
1875CC	250.00	450.00	–
1875S	100.00	225.00	–
1876	275.00	550.00	900.00
1876CC	300.00	500.00	–
1876S	125.00	300.00	–
1877	400.00	800.00	1,400.00
1877CC	275.00	450.00	–
1877S	75.00	150.00	–
1878	45.00	60.00	1,000.00
1878CC	500.00	1,000.00	–
1878S	33.00	36.00	–
1879	33.00	36.00	600.00
1879CC	150.00	300.00	–
1879S	33.00	36.00	–
1880	33.00	36.00	500.00
1880CC	90.00	175.00	–
1880S	33.00	36.00	–
1881	33.00	36.00	400.00
1881CC	100.00	200.00	–
1881S	33.00	36.00	–
1882	33.00	36.00	400.00
1882CC	80.00	125.00	–
1882S	33.00	36.00	–
1883	33.00	36.00	450.00
1883CC	100.00	200.00	–
1883S	33.00	36.00	–
1884	33.00	36.00	800.00
1884CC	100.00	160.00	–
1884S	33.00	60.00	–

	V. Fine	Unc.	Proof
1885	33.00	60.00	400.00
1885S	33.00	60.00	–
1886	33.00	60.00	400.00
1886S	33.00	60.00	–
1887	–	–	2,750.00
1887S	33.00	60.00	–
1888	50.00	80.00	650.00
1888S	33.00	36.00	–
1889	200.00	400.00	700.00
1890	200.00	425.00	700.00
1890CC	55.00	70.00	–
1891	45.00	60.00	500.00
1891CC	50.00	85.00	–
1892	33.00	36.00	450.00
1892CC	50.00	90.00	–
1892O	450.00	750.00	–
1892S	33.00	36.00	–
1893	33.00	36.00	450.00
1893CC	60.00	100.00	–
1893O	60.00	100.00	–
1893S	33.00	36.00	–
1894	33.00	36.00	500.00
1894O	70.00	110.00	–
1894S	50.00	75.00	–
1895	33.00	36.00	450.00
1895S	33.00	36.00	–
1896	33.00	36.00	450.00
1896S	33.00	36.00	–
1897	33.00	36.00	450.00
1897S	33.00	36.00	–
1898	33.00	36.00	425.00
1898S	33.00	36.00	–
1899	33.00	36.00	425.00
1899S	33.00	36.00	–
1900	33.00	36.00	400.00
1900S	33.00	36.00	–
1901	33.00	36.00	400.00
1901S	33.00	36.00	–
1902	33.00	36.00	400.00
1902S	33.00	36.00	–
1903	33.00	36.00	425.00
1903S	33.00	36.00	–
1904	33.00	36.00	425.00
1904S	45.00	75.00	–
1905	33.00	36.00	425.00
1905S	33.00	36.00	–
1906	33.00	36.00	425.00
1906D	33.00	36.00	–
1906S	33.00	36.00	–
1907	33.00	36.00	425.00
1907D	33.00	36.00	–
1908	33.00	36.00	–

INDIAN HEAD TYPE

	V. Fine	Unc.	Proof
1908	51.00	57.00	650.00
1908D	55.00	70.00	–
1908S	150.00	400.00	–
1909	51.00	57.00	700.00
1909D	51.00	57.00	–
1909O	200.00	450.00	–
1909S	51.00	110.00	–
1910	51.00	57.00	700.00
1910D	51.00	110.00	–
1910S	51.00	80.00	–
1911	51.00	80.00	700.00
1911D	100.00	225.00	–
1911S	51.00	65.00	–
1912	51.00	65.00	700.00
1912S	51.00	65.00	–
1913	51.00	65.00	700.00
1913S	51.00	110.00	–
1914	51.00	65.00	800.00
1914D	51.00	65.00	–
1914S	51.00	100.00	–
1915	51.00	65.00	900.00
1915S	51.00	65.00	–
1916S	51.00	65.00	–
1929	1,250.00	1,500.00	–
Complete Collection Indian Head Half Eagles. 24 Pieces	2,725.00	–	–

46.
EAGLES–
1795–1933

($10 GOLD PIECES)

BUST TYPE

1795–1797

1797–1804

	V. Fine	*Unc.*	*Proof*
1795	1,200.00	2,500.00	–
1796	1,000.00	2,200.00	–
1797 Small Eagle	1,300.00	2,500.00	–
1797 Large Eagle	1,000.00	1,400.00	–
1798 over 97, 9 Star Left, 4 Right	1,500.00	3,000.00	–
1798 over 97, 7 Stars Left, 6 Right	3,500.00	7,500.00	–
1799	700.00	1,000.00	–
1800	700.00	1,000.00	–
1801	700.00	1,000.00	–
1803	700.00	1,000.00	–
1804	800.00	1,500.00	–

CORONET TYPE

	V. Fine	Unc.	Proof
1838	500.00	900.00	–
1839	400.00	750.00	–

1840–1865

1866–1907

1840	65.00	200.00	–
1841	60.00	150.00	–
1841O	375.00	800.00	–
1842	55.00	150.00	–
1842O	65.00	200.00	–
1843	50.00	100.00	–
1843O	35.00	110.00	–
1844	200.00	450.00	–
1844O	50.00	150.00	–
1845	60.00	150.00	–
1845O	50.00	150.00	–
1846	65.00	175.00	–
1846O	55.00	110.00	–
1847	50.00	100.00	–
1847O	35.00	100.00	–
1848	50.00	100.00	–
1848O	55.00	125.00	–
1849	50.00	100.00	–
1849O	65.00	175.00	–
1850	50.00	90.00	–
1850O	60.00	150.00	–
1851	50.00	100.00	–
1851O	50.00	100.00	–
1852	50.00	85.00	–

	V. Fine	Unc.	Proof
1852O	100.00	225.00	–
1853	50.00	85.00	–
1853O	75.00	150.00	–
1854	50.00	90.00	–
1854O	80.00	200.00	–
1854S	50.00	125.00	–
1855	50.00	90.00	4,000.00
1855O	100.00	250.00	–
1855S	150.00	325.00	–
1856	50.00	95.00	2,500.00
1856O	70.00	225.00	–
1856S	50.00	150.00	–
1857	100.00	250.00	2,500.00
1857O	250.00	500.00	–
1857S	75.00	250.00	–
1858	3,000.00	6,000.00	–
1858O	75.00	250.00	–
1858S	80.00	200.00	–
1859	100.00	250.00	1,400.00
1859O	200.00	500.00	–
1859S	175.00	400.00	–
1860	75.00	175.00	1,400.00
1860O	75.00	200.00	–
1860S	300.00	500.00	–
1861	50.00	85.00	1,400.00
1861S	75.00	200.00	–
1862	125.00	275.00	1,400.00
1862S	125.00	300.00	–
1863	450.00	900.00	1,600.00
1863S	150.00	400.00	–
1864	250.00	500.00	1,400.00
1864S	400.00	1,000.00	–
1865	250.00	500.00	1,400.00
1865S	300.00	900.00	–
1866	225.00	450.00	–
1866 With Motto	250.00	600.00	1,100.00
1866S	200.00	400.00	–
1867	175.00	400.00	1,000.00
1867S	150.00	250.00	–
1868	100.00	250.00	1,100.00
1868S	100.00	250.00	–
1869	350.00	600.00	1,100.00
1869S	150.00	400.00	–
1870	250.00	450.00	1,000.00
1870CC	300.00	700.00	–
1870S	150.00	300.00	–
1871	250.00	500.00	2,000.00
1871CC	350.00	700.00	–
1871S	100.00	175.00	–
1872	250.00	500.00	1,500.00
1872CC	400.00	700.00	–
1872S	90.00	225.00	–
1873	650.00	1,500.00	2,000.00
1873CC	400.00	750.00	–
1873S	100.00	250.00	–
1874	60.00	100.00	1,800.00
1874CC	150.00	300.00	–

	V. Fine	Unc.	Proof
1874S	125.00	275.00	—
1875	1,000.00	2,000.00	3,500.00
1875CC	300.00	500.00	—
1876	600.00	1,000.00	1,500.00
1876CC	350.00	550.00	—
1876S	225.00	300.00	—
1877	800.00	1,300.00	2,200.00
1877CC	300.00	500.00	—
1877S	65.00	150.00	—
1878	50.00	80.00	1,400.00
1878CC	475.00	800.00	—
1878S	35.00	80.00	—
1879	35.00	80.00	1,000.00
1879CC	800.00	1,200.00	—
1879O	600.00	1,200.00	—
1879S	35.00	80.00	—
1880	35.00	80.00	900.00
1880CC	100.00	175.00	—
1880O	75.00	175.00	—
1880S	35.00	70.00	—
1881	35.00	70.00	900.00
1881CC	90.00	150.00	—
1881O	90.00	200.00	—
1881S	35.00	80.00	—
1882	35.00	80.00	900.00
1882CC	150.00	200.00	—
1882O	70.00	150.00	—
1882S	35.00	70.00	—
1883	35.00	70.00	900.00
1883CC	100.00	200.00	—
1883O	900.00	1,800.00	—
1883S	70.00	150.00	—
1884	35.00	70.00	1,500.00
1884CC	100.00	200.00	—
1884S	35.00	40.00	—
1885	35.00	40.00	800.00
1885S	35.00	40.00	—
1886	35.00	40.00	800.00
1886S	35.00	40.00	—
1887	55.00	75.00	750.00
1887S	35.00	40.00	—
1888	35.00	40.00	750.00
1888O	60.00	125.00	—
1888S	35.00	40.00	—
1889	200.00	400.00	850.00
1889S	35.00	40.00	—
1890	35.00	40.00	750.00
1890CC	60.00	110.00	—
1891	35.00	40.00	750.00
1891CC	50.00	85.00	—
1892	35.00	40.00	850.00
1892CC	60.00	100.00	—
1892O	60.00	90.00	—
1892S	50.00	75.00	—
1893	35.00	40.00	850.00
1893CC	65.00	150.00	—
1893O	55.00	90.00	—

	V. Fine	Unc.	Proof
1893S	35.00	40.00	—
1894	35.00	40.00	900.00
1894O	50.00	75.00	—
1894S	60.00	175.00	—
1895	35.00	40.00	850.00
1895O	35.00	40.00	—
1895S	35.00	40.00	—
1896	35.00	40.00	850.00
1896S	35.00	40.00	—
1897	35.00	40.00	750.00
1897O	35.00	40.00	—
1897S	35.00	40.00	—
1898	35.00	40.00	750.00
1898S	35.00	40.00	—
1899	35.00	40.00	750.00
1899O	35.00	40.00	—
1899S	35.00	40.00	—
1900	35.00	70.00	750.00
1900S	35.00	40.00	—
1901	35.00	40.00	750.00
1901O	35.00	75.00	—
1901S	35.00	40.00	—
1902	35.00	40.00	750.00
1902S	35.00	40.00	—
1903	35.00	40.00	750.00
1903O	35.00	40.00	—
1903S	35.00	40.00	—
1904	35.00	40.00	750.00
1904O	35.00	65.00	—
1905	35.00	40.00	750.00
1905S	35.00	40.00	—
1906	35.00	40.00	750.00
1906D	35.00	40.00	—
1906O	35.00	40.00	—
1906S	35.00	40.00	—
1907 All Kinds	35.00	40.00	750.00
1907D	35.00	40.00	—
1907S	35.00	40.00	—

INDIAN HEAD TYPE

No Motto

Motto

	V. Fine	Unc.	Proof
1907 Wire Edge, Periods before and after Legends	–	2,000.00	3,000.00
1907 Rolled Edge, Periods	–	7,000.00	–
1907 No Periods	60.00	100.00	–
1908 No Motto	60.00	125.00	–
1908D No Motto	60.00	100.00	–
1908 With Motto	60.00	100.00	1,200.00
1908D	60.00	100.00	–
1908S	90.00	275.00	–
1909	60.00	100.00	1,200.00
1909D	60.00	100.00	–
1909S	60.00	100.00	–
1910	60.00	100.00	1,200.00
1910D	60.00	100.00	–
1910S	60.00	100.00	–
1911	60.00	100.00	1,200.00
1911D	100.00	200.00	–
1911S	100.00	200.00	–
1912	60.00	100.00	1,200.00
1912S	60.00	100.00	–
1913	60.00	100.00	1,200.00
1913S	75.00	125.00	–
1914	60.00	100.00	1,200.00
1914D	60.00	100.00	–
1914S	60.00	90.00	–
1915	60.00	90.00	1,400.00
1915S	100.00	200.00	–
1916S	85.00	150.00	–
1920S	2,500.00	4,000.00	–
1926	60.00	90.00	–
1930S	2,200.00	3,500.00	–
1932	60.00	90.00	–
1933	3,000.00	4,500.00	–

47.
DOUBLE EAGLES—
1850–1932

($20 GOLD PIECES)

CORONET TYPE

1849–1865 1866–1907

1894 Unique—U.S. Mint Collection	*V. Fine*	*Unc.*	*Proof*
1850	150.00	400.00	—
1850O	150.00	400.00	—
1851	100.00	200.00	—
1851O	125.00	300.00	—
1852	125.00	200.00	—
1852O	125.00	350.00	—
1853	100.00	200.00	—
1853O	200.00	450.00	—
1854	100.00	200.00	—
1854O	1,750.00	3,500.00	—
1854S	140.00	400.00	—
1855	100.00	200.00	—
1855O	400.00	750.00	—
1855S	100.00	200.00	—
1856	100.00	200.00	—
1856O	4,000.00	7,500.00	—
1856S	110.00	200.00	—
1857	100.00	200.00	—
1857O	250.00	450.00	—
1857S	100.00	200.00	—
1858	100.00	200.00	3,500.00
1858O	300.00	500.00	—
1858S	100.00	200.00	—
1859	200.00	400.00	3,000.00

	V. Fine	Unc.	Proof
1859O	450.00	900.00	–
1859S	125.00	250.00	–
1860	100.00	200.00	2,000.00
1860O	850.00	1,500.00	–
1860S	100.00	175.00	–
1861	100.00	150.00	2,000.00
1861O	500.00	900.00	–
1861S	100.00	200.00	–
1862	200.00	400.00	2,000.00
1862S	100.00	250.00	–
1863	200.00	425.00	2,000.00
1863S	100.00	200.00	–
1864	125.00	250.00	2,000.00
1864S	100.00	200.00	–
1865	150.00	250.00	2,000.00
1865S	100.00	200.00	–
1866	450.00	900.00	–
1866 With Motto	125.00	300.00	2,000.00
1866S	100.00	200.00	–
1867	100.00	200.00	2,000.00
1867S	100.00	200.00	–
1868	150.00	250.00	2,000.00
1868S	100.00	150.00	–
1869	120.00	200.00	2,000.00
1869S	100.00	200.00	–
1870	100.00	250.00	2,000.00
1870CC	5,000.00	9,000.00	–
1870S	100.00	200.00	–
1871	125.00	300.00	2,000.00
1871CC	500.00	900.00	–
1871S	100.00	150.00	–
1872	100.00	200.00	2,000.00
1872CC	300.00	500.00	–
1872S	100.00	150.00	–
1873	100.00	150.00	2,200.00
1873CC	300.00	650.00	–
1873S	90.00	125.00	–
1874	90.00	125.00	2,200.00
1874CC	100.00	175.00	–
1874S	90.00	125.00	–
1875	90.00	125.00	2,200.00
1875CC	100.00	200.00	–
1875S	90.00	125.00	–
1876	90.00	125.00	2,200.00
1876CC	100.00	175.00	–
1876S	90.00	110.00	–
1877	90.00	110.00	2,300.00
1877CC	150.00	200.00	–
1877S	90.00	110.00	–
1878	90.00	110.00	2,300.00
1878CC	200.00	400.00	–
1878S	90.00	110.00	–
1879	90.00	110.00	2,300.00
1879CC	300.00	600.00	–
1879O	600.00	1,200.00	–
1879S	90.00	110.00	–
1880	90.00	125.00	2,000.00

	V. Fine	Unc.	Proof
1880S	90.00	110.00	–
1881	800.00	1,200.00	2,500.00
1881S	90.00	110.00	–
1882	1,200.00	2,500.00	3,500.00
1882CC	100.00	200.00	–
1882S	90.00	110.00	–
1883	–	–	7,500.00
1883CC	150.00	225.00	–
1883S	90.00	125.00	–
1884	–	–	6,500.00
1884CC	150.00	250.00	–
1884S	90.00	110.00	–
1885	1,000.00	2,000.00	4,000.00
1885CC	350.00	600.00	–
1885S	90.00	110.00	–
1886	1,000.00	3,500.00	4,500.00
1887	–	–	4,500.00
1887S	90.00	150.00	–
1888	90.00	150.00	3,000.00
1888S	90.00	110.00	–
1889	100.00	250.00	2,500.00
1889CC	100.00	250.00	–
1889S	90.00	110.00	–
1890	100.00	150.00	2,000.00
1890CC	100.00	200.00	–
1890S	90.00	110.00	–
1891	500.00	1,000.00	2,200.00
1891CC	350.00	600.00	–
1891S	90.00	110.00	–
1892	450.00	850.00	2,100.00
1892CC	150.00	225.00	–
1892S	90.00	110.00	–
1893	90.00	115.00	2,000.00
1893CC	175.00	300.00	–
1893S	60.00	85.00	–
1894	60.00	85.00	2,000.00
1894S	60.00	85.00	–
1895	60.00	85.00	2,000.00
1895S	60.00	85.00	–
1896	60.00	85.00	2,000.00
1896S	60.00	85.00	–
1897	60.00	85.00	2,000.00
1897S	60.00	85.00	–
1898	90.00	120.00	2,000.00
1898S	60.00	85.00	–
1899	60.00	85.00	2,000.00
1899S	60.00	85.00	–
1900	60.00	85.00	2,000.00
1900S	60.00	85.00	–
1901	60.00	85.00	2,100.00
1901S	60.00	85.00	–
1902	100.00	175.00	2,100.00
1902S	60.00	85.00	–
1903	60.00	85.00	1,800.00
1903S	60.00	85.00	–
1904	60.00	85.00	2,000.00
1904S	60.00	85.00	–

	V. Fine	Unc.	Proof
1905	100.00	175.00	2,200.00
1905S	60.00	85.00	–
1906	100.00	150.00	2,100.00
1906D	60.00	85.00	–
1906S	60.00	85.00	–
1907	60.00	85.00	2,100.00
1907D	60.00	85.00	–
1907S	60.00	85.00	–

SAINT-GAUDENS TYPE

	V. Fine	Unc.	Proof
1907 High Relief Roman Numerals (MCMVII) Wire Rim	450.00	900.00	2,500.00
1907 High Relief Flat Rim	450.00	900.00	2,500.00

1907–1908 1908–1932 Motto

	V. Fine	Unc.	Proof
1907 Small Letters on Edge. No Motto	85.00	110.00	–
1908	80.00	100.00	–
1908D	80.00	110.00	–
1908 With Motto	60.00	110.00	2,200.00
1908D	100.00	150.00	–
1908S	150.00	500.00	–
1909 over 8	110.00	200.00	–
1909	100.00	200.00	2,200.00
1909D	110.00	275.00	–
1909S	60.00	85.00	–
1910	60.00	85.00	2,000.00
1910D	60.00	85.00	–
1910S	60.00	85.00	–
1911	60.00	95.00	2,200.00
1911D	60.00	85.00	–

	V. Fine	Unc.	Proof
1911S	60.00	85.00	–
1912	100.00	175.00	2,200.00
1913	60.00	95.00	2,500.00
1913D	60.00	95.00	–
1913S	110.00	250.00	–
1914	60.00	95.00	2,600.00
1914D	60.00	85.00	–
1914S	60.00	85.00	–
1915	60.00	85.00	2,600.00
1915S	60.00	85.00	–
1916S	90.00	125.00	–
1920	60.00	85.00	–
1920S	750.00	1,500.00	–
1921	1,500.00	3,000.00	–
1922	60.00	85.00	–
1922S	125.00	275.00	–
1923	60.00	85.00	–
1923D	60.00	85.00	–
1924	60.00	85.00	–
1924D	125.00	225.00	–
1924S	225.00	375.00	–
1925	60.00	85.00	–
1925D	225.00	500.00	–
1925S	150.00	300.00	–
1926	60.00	85.00	–
1926D	400.00	700.00	–
1926S	150.00	350.00	–
1927	60.00	85.00	–
1927D	600.00	1,200.00	–
1927S	500.00	1,000.00	–
1928	60.00	85.00	–
1929	700.00	1,500.00	–
1930S	1,000.00	2,500.00	–
1931	900.00	1,800.00	–
1931D	1,500.00	3,000.00	–
1932	750.00	2,000.00	–

48.

PRIVATE AND TERRITORIAL GOLD COINS

GEORGIA

1830 $2.50 TEMPLETON REID (Very rare) ....
1830 $5.00 TEMPLETON REID (Very rare) ....
1830 TEN DOLLARS (Very rare) ....
NO DATE, TEN DOLLARS (Very rare) ....

NORTH CAROLINA

	Fine	Unc.
$1.00 CHRISTOPHER BECHTLER	125.00	225.00
$2.50	300.00	500.00
$5.00	350.00	500.00
$5.00 AUGUST BECHTLER	350.00	500.00

CALIFORNIA

NORRIS, GRIEG AND NORRIS

1849 $5.00	500.00	1,000.00

MOFFAT & CO.

	Fine	Ex. Fine	–
1849 $10.00	500.00	700.00	–
1849 $5.00	300.00	350.00	–
1850 $5.00	300.00	475.00	–
1852 $10.00	600.00	800.00	–

AUGUSTUS HUMBERT

U. S. ASSAYER

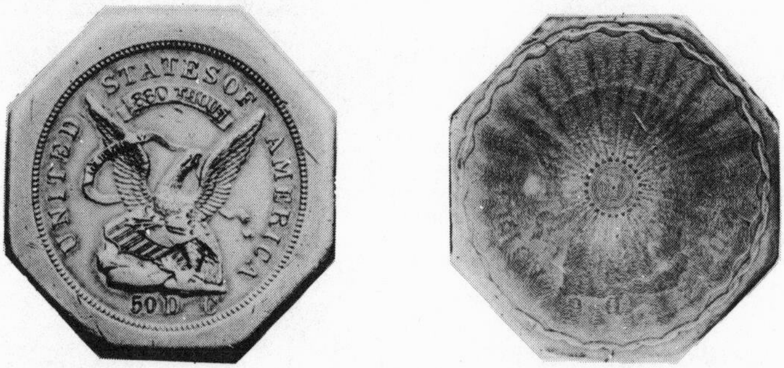

1851 FIFTY DOLLARS 880 THOUS. "Target" Reverse	2,500.00	3,500.00	–
1851 FIFTY DOLLARS 887 THOUS. "Target" Reverse	2,750.00	3,750.00	–
1852 FIFTY DOLLARS 887 THOUS. No "Target"	1,750.00	2,250.00	–
1852 FIFTY DOLLARS 900 THOUS.	1,850.00	2,500.00	–
1851 50 D Several Varieties: AUGUSTUS HUMBERT UNITED STATES ASSAYER OF GOLD CALIFORNIA 1851	2,500.00	3,500.00	–
1852 TWENTY DOLLARS 1852 over 1	2,500.00	3,500.00	–
1853 TWENTY DOLLARS 884 THOUS.	1,750.00	2,000.00	–
1853 TWENTY DOLLARS 900 THOUS.	400.00	500.00	–

	Fine	Ex. Fine	
1852 TEN DOLLARS 1852 over 1	400.00	600.00	–
1852 TEN DOLLARS 884 THOUS.	750.00	1,000.00	–
1853 TEN DOLLARS 884 THOUS.	700.00	900.00	–
1853 TEN DOLLARS 900 THOUS.	700.00	1,000.00	–

BALDWIN & COMPANY

	Fine	Unc.	
1850 TEN DOLLARS	3,750.00	7,500.00	–
1851 TWENTY DOLLARS	4,000.00	8,000.00	–
1851 TEN DOLLARS	3,000.00	4,000.00	–
1850 FIVE DOLLARS	1,000.00	1,250.00	–

SCHULTZ & COMPANY

1851 FIVE DOLLARS	5,000.00	10,000.00	–

DUNBAR & COMPANY

1851 FIVE DOLLARS	*Ex. Fine*	12,000.00	–

WASS, MOLITOR & COMPANY

	Fine	Ex. Fine	—
1855 FIFTY DOLLARS	2,500.00	4,500.00	—
1855 TWENTY DOLLARS, Small Head	1,000.00	2,000.00	—
1855 TWENTY DOLLARS, Large Head	3,000.00	5,000.00	—
1852 TEN DOLLARS, Small Head	700.00	1,500.00	—
1852 TEN DOLLARS, Large Head	300.00	600.00	—
1855 TEN DOLLARS	600.00	1,200.00	—
1852 FIVE DOLLARS, Small Head	600.00	1,000.00	—
1852 FIVE DOLLARS, Large Head	500.00	900.00	—

KELLOGG & COMPANY

1855 FIFTY DOLLARS	2,000.00	4,000.00	—
1854 TWENTY DOLLARS	300.00	500.00	—
1855 TWENTY DOLLARS	300.00	550.00	—

There were also issued, in California, round and octagonal twenty-five-cent, fifty-cent, and one-dollar gold pieces of which there are many copies and "charms." Genuine pieces must have their denomination upon them, i.e. "½ Dol.," or "½ Dollar," or "half dollar," etc. These coins are valued as follows:

	Fine	*Unc.*	–
.25 Round Indian or Liberty Heads	16.00	30.00	–
.25 Octagonal Indian or Liberty Heads	16.00	30.00	–
.50 Round Indian or Liberty Heads	17.50	35.00	–
.50 Octagonal Indian or Liberty Heads	17.50	35.00	–
1.00 Round Indian Heads	50.00	90.00	–
1.00 Octagonal Indian or Liberty Heads	50.00	90.00	–
1.00 Round Liberty Heads (Rare)	250.00	600.00	–

OREGON

OREGON EXCHANGE COMPANY

	Fine	*Ex. Fine*	*V. Fine*
1849 TEN DOLLARS	–	–	10,500.00
1849 FIVE DOLLARS	2,000.00	3,000.00	–

UTAH

MORMON GOLD

1849 TWENTY DOLLARS	*V. Fine*	6,500.00
1849 TEN DOLLARS	*Fine*	14,000.00

	Fine	Ex. Fine	
1849 FIVE DOLLARS	400.00	600.00	—

1849 TWO AND ONE HALF DOLLARS	500.00	850.00	—
1850 FIVE DOLLARS	400.00	600.00	—

1860 FIVE DOLLARS	750.00	1,500.00	—

COLORADO

CLARK, GRUBER & COMPANY

1860 TWENTY DOLLARS	—	5,000.00	—
1860 TEN DOLLARS	750.00	1,750.00	—
1861 TWENTY DOLLARS	1,000.00	2,000.00	—

1861 TEN DOLLARS	400.00	550.00	—
1861 FIVE DOLLARS	400.00	600.00	—
1861 TWO AND ONE HALF DOLLARS	300.00	500.00	—

CLARK & CO.

1860 FIVE DOLLARS	400.00	550.00	—
1860 TWO AND ONE HALF DOLLARS	350.00	550.00	—

JOHN PARSONS & COMPANY

(1861) Undated 2 ½ D	3,000.00	5,000.00	—
(1861) Undated FIVE D	5,000.00	8,000.00	—

J. J. CONWAY & COMPANY

(1861) 2 ½ DOLL'S	—	13,500.00	—
(1861) FIVE DOLLARS	—	10,000.00	—
1861 TEN DOLLARS (Very rare)	—	—	—

49.

THE CENTS OF 1793

The collecting of large cents is called the Grandad of all coin collecting and represents one of the most fascinating series of United States coins.

First minted in 1793, when George Washington was president, they had an obverse design of Liberty's head with flowing hair facing right and a reverse design with a circle of chains (presumably to represent unity) around "one Cent" and the legend, "United States of AMERI," which soon became "United States of America," the latter having a variety with and without a period after the date.

Also in 1793 the chain gave way to a wreath on the reverse. The wreath type first had a vine and bars on the edge, and then a lettered edge with the legend "one hundred for a dollar."

An experimental strawberry leaf on the wreath type was minted but these were considered patterns and were not issued for regular circulation.

Some of the unflattering nicknames for the early cents were "Frightened Liberty," "A running Squaw," "Liberty in Chains." These prompted many of the changes.

Toward the end of the year, the "Liberty and Cap" appeared. The "Cap" idea was undoubtedly inspired by the cap of Freedom popular in France during the French Revolution. It was short-lived, however, and replaced in 1796 by the bust type. All the cents of the year 1793 are rare.

50.

THE UNLUCKY THREES

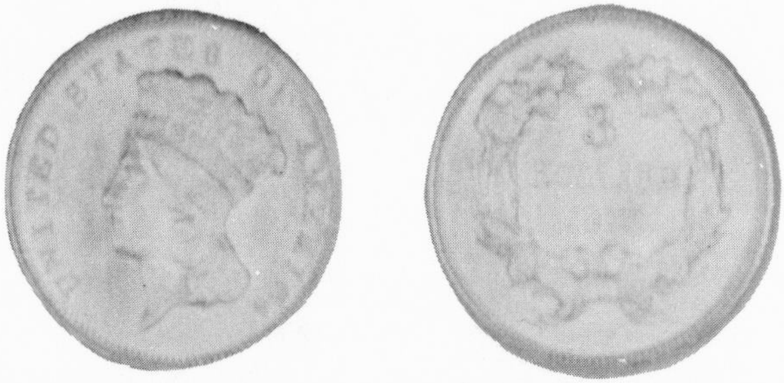

The innovation of three-cent postage stamps, sold by the government, led to the issue of silver three-cent and gold three-dollar pieces in 1853 and 1854. The three-cent pieces were designed to purchase one stamp, the three-dollar gold pieces designed to purchase a sheet of one hundred stamps.

Due to their size, the silver three-cents were replaced with an alloyed coin in 1865, the three-cent nickel. The silver coins' smallness had made them unpopular. These were finally discontinued in 1873.

The nickel pieces became unpopular because of their similarity in size and design to dimes.

Three-dollar gold pieces were never popular, being very similar in size to Half Eagles. This caused them to be frequently mistaken for them.

Add to their unpopularity a change in postage rates, and we see why all were discontinued in 1889 to become the black sheep of our monetary system.

It has only been in the last few decades that numismatists realized the limited number of gold threes that had been coined and appreciated their rarity.

51.

THE NEW EISENHOWER DOLLAR

The new Eisenhower dollar has been approved and orders will be accepted on and after July 1, 1971. Applications for orders will be available in U.S. Post Offices. Proof dollars will be available at $10 each, and uncirculated dollars at $3 each. The maximum order for both coins is five to a customer. These will be struck in silver. Later on, a clad dollar will be issued through the banks at face value. All deliveries should be made by the end of 1971.